"This book tells truth and tells it well. I recommend it."
—Marianne Williamson

"These simple steps can lead to a peaceful and meaningful life. Casey's self-help book is a winner!"
—Frederic Brussat, spiritualityandpractice.com

"This book is a must-read for anyone who cares about the quality of their thoughts and how being aware of them can bring positive change."
—Mary Porter, *Science of Mind*

"This book is small, is easy to digest, and would likely be taken from the display shelf by someone needing a psychological boost."
—Deborah Bigelow, *Library Journal*

"This book is an absolutely wonderful, magical, and deeply transforming book. It is a small book that can have a big impact. It inspires, guides, and challenges as it provides a practical design for living."
—Tian Dayton, author of *Emotional Sobriety*

"Casey's voice is thoughtful and accessible. Readers with a belief in the power of God will be most amenable to her recommendations for a simpler, more rewarding life."
—Publisher's Weekly

Change Your Mind and Your Life Will Follow

Other Books by Karen Casey

Each Day a New Beginning
Each Day a Renewed Beginning
Each Day a New Beginning: Journal
It's Up to You
Let Go Now
Codepenence and the Power of Detachment
52 Ways to Live the Course in Miracles
Living Long, Living Passionately
All We Have Is All We Need
Peace a Day At a Time
The Language of Healing
20 Things I Know for Sure
The Good Stuff from Growing Up in a Dysfunctional Family
Getting Unstuck
My Story to Yours
Cultivating Hope
Be Who You Wanna Be
Serenity
The Miracle of Sponsorship
The Promise of a New Day
Fearless Relationships
Girls Only
Girl to Girl
Daily Meditations for Practicing the Course
Keepers of the Wisdom
A Woman's Spirit
A Life of My Own
In God's Care
If Only I Could Quit
Worthy of Love

Change Your Mind and Your Life Will Follow

Master Your Mindset
with 12 Simple Principles

Karen Casey

Conari
Press

Coral Gables

For permission requests, please contact the publisher at:
Mango Publishing Group
2850 S Douglas Road, 2nd Floor
Coral Gables, FL 33134 USA
info@mango.bz

For special orders, quantity sales, course adoptions and corporate sales, please email the publisher at sales@mango.bz. For trade and wholesale sales, please contact Ingram Publisher Services at customer.service@ingramcontent.com or +1.800.509.4887.

Change Your Mind and Your Life Will Follow: Master Your Mindset with 12 Simple Principles

Library of Congress Cataloging-in-Publication number: 2022943088
ISBN: (pb) 978-1-68481-100-7, (hc) 978-1-68481-301-8,
     (e) 978-1-68481-101-4
BISAC category code SEL029000, SELF-HELP / Twelve-Step Programs

Printed in the United States of America

TABLE OF CONTENTS

A PREFACE REVISITED

It's a bit mind-bending realizing that *Change Your Mind and Your Life Will Follow* was written over a decade ago. I was sitting right where I am now, in our Minnesota lake home, pounding away on my Apple computer in the wee hours of the morning.

I had a deadline that I intended to make, and the ideas filled my mind as quickly as I was able to make space for them. The words tumbled forth almost unnoticed by me. And the ideas kept coming.

Gloriously I sat among the ideas and the thousands of words knowing, without question, that I was doing exactly what I was intended to do. That's been the beauty of my writing life, actually. I have never doubted that the "God of my understanding" had called me to attention as I sat before my computer. In fact, that "god" had first called me to attention in 1981 as I sat, not many miles from here, with pen and legal pad in hand, writing the words that were to become my first book: *Each Day a New Beginning*. My "god" has kept me very busy over the years, listening and then writing the hundreds of thousands of words that have filled many books. I consider myself a lucky woman indeed.

As I sit here recalling the many pleasures, as well as the struggles, of my life, I am wholeheartedly convinced that I wouldn't change any single event. I believe that every one of them wore my name. Whomever I met I know agreed to meet me. Whatever I learned was on the list I came here to sort out. Having this mindset gives me relief beyond measure. It has allowed me to trust that whatever remains of my life will be exactly as it is destined to be. And all who cross my path want to do so. We will meet because that has been our intention. We will learn that which we came here to learn.

Reviewing this book you now hold a full decade after it was first published pleases me, not only because of the message that I continue to feel committed to word for word, but because it has stood this brief test of time. I simply wouldn't change a word of this book, with the exception of updating the number of sober years I have had, and that seems remarkable, actually. Is it because I got the message so right the first time around or because I trust that what was written then simply needed to be shared by me in that perfect time? And what I may need to share now will find its way onto the pages of another book.

My journey with you, the reader, has been such a gift, one that I feel so blessed to have traveled. That we have been able to develop a friendship through this and perhaps other books of mine, too, has given my life such a rich purpose. We each have been purposefully born. I relish this Truth.

Day in and day out. That it will pull me forward into my next pursuit allows my breath to freely escape between my softened lips. We are here by intention. We will be "there" with intention too.

May your every step be taken with as much assurance as your heart can hold. And may we meet repeatedly along this journey that has so lovingly called our names.

Karen Casey
www.womens-spirituality.com

INTRODUCTION

My Journey

I am daughter number three. Sixty-five years ago my father, against the doctor's advice, insisted that my mother get pregnant again. He wanted a son. My mother didn't want any more children. I can't be certain that I sensed her unhappiness about my impending birth while in the womb, but I think I did. A former therapist of mine thinks so, too. Two years after I was born, there was a fourth child, a son. My dad rejoiced. My mom became even sadder.

My earliest memories are of closely watching my parents' every move, trying to figure out if I was the cause of their unhappiness, of my dad's incessant rage and my mother's sadness. Watching their faces for clues about how I should feel and behave became second nature to me. And I strenuously avoided eye contact with either of them.

Most of the time I was scared. At times the fear was immobilizing. I spent many Sunday afternoons and evenings on the living room couch, sick to the point of vomiting, because I had to go back to school on Monday morning and face teachers who made me as fearful and uncomfortable as my parents did. My fear followed me throughout childhood and into adulthood, stomach aches and all.

By the time I was in high school the habits I had formed to deal with my anxiety—including escaping into a fantasy world, which I wrote about during spare moments—were well-honed. I wanted to spend as little time as possible around my real family, so I lied about my age and got a job in a department store when I was barely fifteen. I went to work every day after school and on Saturdays, thus managing to greatly reduce the number of hours a week that I had to interact with my family.

Unfortunately this did nothing for my anxiety.

Growing up, my siblings and I never talked about the near-constant fighting at our house. Sadly, we seldom talked to each other at all, so I never knew if the fighting triggered the same kind of fear in them. It seemed that each one of us more or less tiptoed around the house, trying to avoid my dad's wrath, without ever acknowledging that that was what we were doing. Perhaps our isolation from one another was our attempt to keep the fear from "being real" and overtaking us.

Only in the last few years have my siblings and I broached the topic of the tension in our household. Since no two people ever share the same perceptions in "troubled families" it's perhaps not surprising that no one seems to recall it as vividly as I do. One sister hardly recalls it at all.

Throughout high school, even though I was a member of the "in group," I always felt slightly separate. I often tried to read the faces of my friends to see how well I was liked, as had been my steady habit in my family. I am quite certain that none of my friends realized how insecure I felt. I certainly never voiced my fears. I didn't need to. By age fifteen I had discovered the perfect anxiety reducer: alcohol.

My drinking was alcoholic from the start. I didn't get drunk every day, of course. It was not until I was married that I started drinking every day. But I did feel an immediate sense of well-being every time I drank, and I loved the freedom from fear that alcohol offered me. My love of alcohol didn't elicit reprimands or even a glance from my parents. They drank, too, as did all of their friends, as well as their siblings. It was easy to indulge without drawing attention to myself. And luckily for me there were frequent family gatherings where I managed to meld into the woodwork with a drink in one hand and a stolen cigarette in the other.

In 1957, I reluctantly entered college, with just one purpose in mind—to find a husband who wanted to party. I had not actually put words to my intent, but it was evident to anyone who watched. And I succeeded. My first marriage, which began while we were seniors at Purdue University, quite surprisingly lasted twelve years. Alcohol was first the glue and then the poison.

We had not set out to hurt one another, but we did.

Over and over again.

Long before the marriage ended, we moved to Minnesota in order for my husband to attend graduate school. The pain of our lives escalated because of the alcohol and my husband's infidelities. By the time we divorced, my alcoholism was out of control, but I was miraculously mastering the art of attending graduate school myself. With hindsight, I marvel at how easily I moved through my PhD program. I certainly had not come to Minnesota with any plan to pursue a graduate degree. But alcohol fueled my confidence and, with nothing better to do and no real plan for my life, I enrolled. I am certain that had I not been drinking at the time, I would not have attempted graduate school. I had been an elementary school teacher for eight years in Indiana and Minnesota and doubted that I was smart enough to do anything else. No one was more surprised than I when I began accumulating As. But my fears still controlled me. I had not escaped my need for constant attention and affirmation from others, particularly men. It's fortunate that drinking finally quit doing for me what I needed it to do. By giving up alcohol and other drugs in 1976, I was able to salvage a life that was literally headed for a dead end.

Change Your Mind and Your Life Will Follow

Getting sober has made me profoundly aware that there are no accidents. Where we are, where I am right now, is intentional. The same can be said for you, of course.

The development of this perspective evolved over a number of years, years spent not only in the exploration of numerous spiritual pathways but also in an attempt to listen to the inner voice, which I believe to be the source of all knowledge. This perspective, that everything we need to know lies within us, has explained and eased every aspect of my life. It has informed my decisions. It has led me to write and publish sixteen books in twenty years.

The book you are now holding reveals another, deeper layer to this belief in the power of perspective. It is claimed that Abe Lincoln once said, "We are as happy as we make up our minds to be." I like this idea. It simplifies our assignment. We can have better lives if we make up our minds to do so. The choice is ours. Wherever we go, there we are, as the people we have decided to be.

We decide. That's the revelation. We decide if we are going to live lives that are bitter or sweet. We decide, in every moment, to respond from peace or from fear. We decide.

The truth is it doesn't take very much effort to make our lives "sweeter." It does take willingness, though—willingness to make tiny shifts in how we perceive our experiences and our fellow travelers. Instead of perceiving everyone and everything as a potential threat or obstacle, we can choose to approach each moment as an opportunity to be peaceful.

And each time we choose the peaceful response, we are paving the way not only for our own happiness but for a peaceful world as well. In this book I will teach you the twelve principles that can help us manifest a peaceful world. Just twelve simple principles to practice. That's all. Won't you join me?

CHAPTER 1

Tend Your Own Garden

It's easy to make other people the focus of our attention, isn't it? Women, especially, are raised to do so.

We judge, we criticize, sometimes audibly; through anger, manipulation, shame, or guilt, we try to control the people sharing our journey. I have news for you. These are always wrong choices and never "the work" we have been called to do.

Focusing outside ourselves and attempting to control other people is a clever avoidance technique; temporarily, at least, it helps us escape having to look at our own sometimes troubling behavior. The irony is that we always see in others the very behaviors that we need to pay some attention to in ourselves. Always!

The people in our lives—family and friends, neighbors, even the strangers at the grocery or ahead of us in the traffic jam—are mirrors that reveal who we are. Our reactions to them show us what we need to work on in ourselves, and as we release them to live their own lives, we can get back to the business of controlling the only thing we really can control: our own responses to life.

Okay, but how? Simple. We have to learn some new behaviors and then practice them.

Cultivating New Behaviors

Attend to Your Life, No One Else's!

Many of us acquired the habit of interfering in other people's affairs early on in life. We heard our parents speaking critically about their friends, or other family members, or neighbors, for their actions or opinions. Obsessively watching the behavior of friends, family, or even complete strangers, and longing to change or control their behavior, is a great catalyst for inner turmoil. This goes hand in hand with the misguided idea that we can change anyone but ourselves. You can spend years trying to change a spouse or some other friend, but what a relief to finally learn that the affairs of others are not ours to control or even to judge. Being in charge of ourselves is enough.

It bears repeating: We are not in charge of others! Not their behavior, their thoughts, their dreams, their problems, their successes, or their failures.

Even the children we parent have their own journey to make, and our so-called control over them is, in fact, an illusion. We can set an example for them, we can suggest a set of behaviors, we can demonstrate a code of ethics, we can even require that they live by certain "house rules" while under our roof, but finally it is they who will decide who they want to be and what they want to do, regardless of our efforts. And for that we will become grateful in time.

I say: Let's celebrate the fact that we are in charge of no one but ourselves. It relieves us of a heavy burden, and a thankless job, one that never blesses us. Taking control of every thought we have and every action we take, and being willing to relinquish the past while savoring the present, will assuredly keep us as busy as we need to be. Doing these things, and only these things, is why we are here. It's only when we live our own lives and manage our own affairs, freeing others to do the same, that we will we find the peace we seek and so deserve.

Let Go and Let Others Be Themselves

So many of us spend countless hours or weeks or, in some sad cases, years, trying to make someone be who we want them to be or do what we think is in their own (or perhaps our) best interests, only to repeatedly fail in our attempts. This is a tragedy as well as a misspent life. It's time to let go.

I was first introduced to the idea of "letting go" in a Twelve Step support group, and I was very slow to grasp the meaning. Wasn't it my job to guide a loved one's decisions and actions? To control them if I could? I had always thought that not doing so was selfish and uncaring. Thankfully what I finally learned was that our spouses, our friends, our family, our neighbors, even the strangers crossing our paths, must be who they are, not who we think they should be. They must make their own mistakes and, through what they learn, have reason to celebrate their own successes.

There are many reasons for letting go of this futile behavior, but the most important ones are that we will never succeed in controlling others and never experience peace in our own lives if we are always focused on how other people are living or how we think they should be living. If we want to be peaceful, we must let go of how others choose to live and take care of business in one life only: our own.

Get Out of the Center of Other People's Lives

Just as no one else can productively or peacefully be the total focus of our lives, we cannot waste precious time thinking we are or should be the center of someone else's life either. That may come as a blow to your ego, but it's time to learn this important truth. This does not mean we should quit interacting with people or shut them out in order to preempt being shut out. Nor does it mean we should ignore how other people are thinking and behaving for fear we will seek an unhealthy dependency on them. Observing others can be both edifying and enlightening.

It simply means getting perspective on our role in all interactions, and understanding where our responsibility for action ends and the other person's begins. Becoming entangled in other people's actions, dreams, or dramas binds us to them in emotionally unhealthy ways and prevents the growth we deserve. Unfortunately, many of us mistake being enmeshed for feeling safe. We want people around us who will pay us constant attention, who will make no plans that don't include us, have no thoughts that aren't shared. But that's not relationship, that's dependence; it is unholy connection. Relationships that truly bring us to peace are interdependent. They allow us to connect while still living and honoring our own lives and letting our "learning partners" do the same.

Take No Hostages

Many of us think our most meaningful work has to do with minding other people's business. Why is it so hard to let other people have their own journey? Why do we persist in interfering in other people's lives, especially when we reap so few benefits? Because our parents did it is not reason enough. We no doubt observed our parents doing many things that we have chosen to avoid. No, there must be another reason.

After nearly three decades of emotional and spiritual growth through Twelve Step programs and other spiritual pathways,

I have concluded that we mind other people's business, we "take hostages," so to speak, strictly out of our own insecurity. We get personally invested in other people and the outcomes of their actions because we see those outcomes as defining our lives in some way, as taking from us or adding to us some heretofore unrealized value.

How sad that we perceive our own well-being as so tied to the decisions, even occasional whims, of others. But we do it, again and again, and our lives are never better for it, at least in the long run. In the short run, trying to help a loved one live his or her life may seem like the right thing to do—it may even be engaging for a while—but taking charge of our own lives is as much work as any one of us needs to experience. The work of someone else's life belongs to that person and God.

In fact, thinking of God, if even just occasionally, in the midst of all our experiences—those that involve others and those that involve us alone—can change our perspective entirely. No experience is mystifying for long if we remember who is orchestrating it.

It is important to remember, of course, that accepting that God is in charge of everyone's life doesn't mean we have nothing to do. Indeed, footwork, some seemingly trivial and some quite specific and elaborate, is always necessary. We must be accountable in our own lives, moment by moment, and demonstrate this by doing the next right thing, but God is ever-present to guide us and everyone else too. Never is any one of us "out of his/her range."

CHAPTER 2

Stop Focusing on Problems So Their Solutions Can Emerge

Lots of folks think that they need to attack their problems in order to resolve them. They will study a problem, analyze it from myriad angles, troubleshoot it, utilize so-called problem-solving techniques that may have appeared successful before, without realizing that within every problem lies its solution. That's right. Problems are only as big and as real as we make them. In fact, they only exist if we allow our egos to create them and then we feed them through our incessant attention.

Take a look at the following suggestions for changing how you look at the "imagined problems" in your life. And never doubt that by changing your mind, you can change every experience in your life.

Cultivating New Behaviors

Quit Making a Big Deal Out of Ordinary Situations

Okay, sounds good, but what's an "ordinary" situation? Being placed on interminable "hold" while trying to find out why a package has not arrived, for example; seeking help when your computer crashes in the middle of a project for work; dealing with a house remodeling project that is woefully behind schedule, and the workmen have failed to make an appearance for more than a week; getting in the wrong line at the grocery, the one where the three people ahead of you forgot an item and had to run back to get it, causing you to be late to meet a friend or to pick up your child from day care. And let's not forget the traffic jam, particularly when you are already running late. All of these extremely ordinary situations can become big problems if we let them. But we don't have to let them.

The only real problem situations are the ones that place our lives in jeopardy, and even those might be perceived as opportunities for new growth.

I remember a very wise man I taught with at the University of Minnesota saying that he used every traffic jam as an opportunity to pray for all of the people in all of the cars ahead of him. He said it immediately changed how he felt. He also had the feeling that his prayers helped to loosen up traffic, too. One can never know if that's objectively true, but simply feeling better from taking an action like prayer whenever one experiences "a problem" makes doing it worthwhile. Prayer certainly never hurts a situation or a person. Quite the contrary. Let's make the decision to joyfully accept all situations—the lines, the traffic jams, the downed computers, and the rest—as opportunities to include God in our lives, in that moment, and then wait for the change in perception that will assuredly come.

Our lives change when our perceptions change. This is an absolute that we can count on!

Stop Overreacting

Many years ago, as I was finishing up in the PhD program at the University of Minnesota, I had a really frightening experience that taught me something about overreacting. All I needed was to get my dissertation approved by all five professors who sat on my committee. Four of the members approved it in a timely fashion. The fifth professor dragged his feet. Naturally, I assumed he was not going to approve it, but I couldn't even get him to make an appointment with me.

My dissertation advisor suggested I set a date for my orals anyway. I did and then pleaded with the "holdout" to meet with me. He finally agreed and I went to his office, a bit fearful but hopeful. His first words were, "This has got to be rewritten." I was stunned and terrified. I sat quite still for a moment, trying to collect my thoughts, which were bouncing from one scary scenario to another. I wanted to scream, call him horrible names, and run from his office. I wanted to shame him, since four of his colleagues had already approved my work in glowing terms and within the appropriate time line.

But before saying anything, I took a deep breath and then a miracle occurred. Some force within me took over my thoughts and I quietly suggested to him that we review his objections together. I was not sure where those words came from. Only moments before I had wanted to scream obscenities and run. But I remained calm. I didn't overreact. In fact, I didn't even react. I simply responded to his "attack" calmly.

What happened next was that we went through every one of his concerns in the three-hundred-page dissertation, and I addressed each one with explanations I didn't even actually hear. I could never have repeated them. Nor could I tell my husband one word I had said when I got home. It felt like an out-of-body experience. I watched myself explain away his criticisms and, three and a half hours later, he approved my work in glowing terms.

I left his office exhilarated but very confused. I knew I didn't know how to answer his questions. But somewhere within me the answers did reside. Had I fallen back on old habits and overreacted to his charge, I might never have received my degree. But I learned two important things from this experience that were, in fact, worth more than the PhD:

1. I learned that remaining calm can help defuse a situation and feelings of terror.

2. I learned that I had the capability to listen to an Inner Wisdom if I chose to.

I have never forgotten the feeling I had when I left his office. Nor have I ever forgotten that our answers are always within. What I have forgotten far too many times, though, is to turn to that source when I most need it.

Making the decision to give up overreacting will ensure us of far smoother relations with others; it will pave the way for a peacefulness we may not have experienced except on rare occasions in the past, and it will open the door to the wisdom that lies within each of us. And if we can't give up our habit of overreacting in every situation, stopping ourselves from overreacting even once a day will impact our lives and all of our relationships in a way we'd never have anticipated. The change isn't just in us. It affects everyone we touch.

Do Nothing

When someone gets "in our face" or attacks us in any way, the desire to retaliate can be nearly overwhelming. My own past is riddled with scenarios where I put on my armor and responded with a vicious attack—frequently an attack far worse than the one that had been directed at me. My dad and I so easily got trapped in this "dance." Every attack on me, my brother, or my mom incited me to rage. There were no winners. My mom was not helped by my behavior. Nor was my brother or I. In every case, whatever justification I felt at the time quickly dissipated. It was generally followed by mortification, shame, embarrassment, or worse. Never did I feel good about my response after I reviewed it in my mind. But seldom was I willing to apologize.

It never occurred to me that being "attacked," verbally or perhaps even physically, didn't necessitate a response. Maybe I needed to remove myself from the situation or even seek the help of the authorities, but I did not have to respond. What a relief when I finally realized this! I had so many opportunities to practice this, to walk away—with my dad, my first husband, my boss of many years. And until I got well into recovery from addictions, I missed every one of these opportunities. Not once did I interpret an attack as a sign of fear on the part of the perpetrator. But that's often precisely what it is.

In my youth, I thought that walking away would be perceived as giving in, and I wanted to make sure my point was understood. But walking away doesn't mean agreeing with your adversary. On the contrary, it means nothing more than that you have made the choice to disengage. These days, I actually relish every opportunity to let a situation pass me by that would have engaged my ire in the past. I feel empowered every time I make this choice. The older I get the more I realize that no circumstance is helped by my anger; very few situations actually endanger me or my life, and I will never know peace if I let myself get trapped in meaningless bickering. Once you look at things this way, you realize that there is precious little in our lives that doesn't fall into this "not life-threatening" category. When all is said and done, doing nothing is often the most helpful thing you can "do"—for all concerned.

Disengage from the Chaos

I remember attending a family wedding where the groom's side of the family made up the majority of the guests. The combination of alcohol and testosterone led to fights, many tears, and the arrival of cops. While the chaos was real, I realized I didn't have to contribute to its escalation. Staying in the drama would only have meant filling my mind with the chaos as well. Those of us who wanted to simply left, giving over the evening to those who wanted to continue the drama. Most chaos is a product of some past, oftentimes imagined slight. One way to free yourself from chaos is to try to stay present in the moment, to not layer an experience with the emotions of memorable chaotic past experiences as well. But this takes real vigilance. Our minds so easily gravitate toward old experiences—or at least what we thought we experienced—as a way of interpreting or anticipating what might come next. If the memory is of something chaotic, we will naturally expect the same this time around and thus increase the chances of actually creating that anticipated chaos in the here and now.

For instance, if there was frequent bickering in your family of origin, if there was far more chaos than peace, you undoubtedly carry this set of expectations into your significant relationships today. But you can make another choice. That's the heartening news for those of us on a spiritual path. We don't have to do what we always did! We don't have to think the way we always thought. We don't have to expect what we always expected.

Our minds are as free of the chaotic past as we choose to make them—which of course means we do not have to engage in the chaos of anyone who is walking on our path at the present time. Our avoidance of chaos can also be a great lesson for others. No one has to be sucked into chaos and drama, but many have yet to learn this.

Disengagement can become a habit just as easily as misguided involvement has been for many of us. It's a mindset, really, an opportunity to change our mind and discover that our life will follow in a new, more peaceful direction. And every habit requires practice. Most of us are more than willing to give our bad habits a lot of practice. Now we have an opportunity to try a new approach—to give the disengagement habit some practice, too. Nothing is stopping you; all it takes is a little willingness.

So What?

I'll never forget what it felt like when a good friend said "So what?" to me one day on the phone. I had called her to complain, once again, about a relationship problem I was having. I had turned to her dozens of times for consolation, for validation of my injured feelings. And she had always been willing to listen. This time, however, she cut me off, and I was insulted, hurt, angry, and really mystified by her response. How could she do this? What about our friendship?

I didn't confront her or tell her how hurt I was, but after stewing over it for a couple of hours I began to laugh. It suddenly dawned on me that she was trying to say "Get over it," whatever "it" was. She was trying to disengage from my constant complaining and in the process show me that I could also disengage from the situations I let rule my thinking.

I realized that I almost always called her over some imagined slight that I then exaggerated. Within our relationships many of us all too easily look for evidence of inattention rather than notice the love that is present. Sure, in some instances I might have been treated unlovingly, but isn't the retort, "So what?" more sensible than getting into the ditch with me? In hindsight, I think so.

Early in my present marriage, one that has lovingly lasted for more than twenty-five years, I used to watch closely for signs of my husband's love and sought near-constant examples of his attention. My husband and I were both trying to figure out how to do a marriage, and at least initially our methods weren't very similar. He had grown up in a family where little attention was ever given to any one child, perhaps because there were eight of them. I had grown up in a family where rage was prevalent. We were like two ships passing in the dark. I was afraid of my "invisibility." He was unsure of how to show his attention. Obviously we learned how to meet halfway. But it wasn't without some pain, lots of patience, and a commitment to staying the course.

I also learned the value of "So what?" I came to realize that most of the issues in my marriage and in the rest of my life didn't require dissection.

I know that my life journey is about learning how to handle situations that baffled me in my youth. I know that the people who have accompanied me on this journey, everyone from the supposed perpetrators of slights to the friend who said "So what?" have been part of the grand scheme of my life. I'm willing to bet this is true for you, too. I know also that the painful earlier periods of my life—my childhood, my first marriage, my cycle of addiction—have all been necessary contributors to the woman I have become.

Looking back on any one experience, or all of them for that matter, I see that I might well have said, "So what?" to any one of them. No experience was out to destroy me. My mind was the culprit. I let it rule my emotions and far too often my actions. Had I known as a child or even as a young adult what I was eventually able to glean from my good friend's comment, I might have saved myself hours upon hours of wallowing in self-pity. You always have the choice between hanging on and letting go. Next time you're beginning to feel overly victimized by life, practice saying, "So what?" to yourself and feel the anxiety drop away.

CHAPTER 3

Let Go of Outcomes

No matter what we do or how perfect our input, the fact is, we are never in control of the outcome of any situation. How elusive this idea often is. Even when we know that we cannot count on a particular result, we tend to expect things to turn out as we'd planned. And when they don't, we will look for someone to blame. Some of us are terrific at blaming ourselves and then feeling unnecessary guilt or shame. That's how hard it is to believe that outcomes are not controllable.

It's probably the human condition to assume that what happened in the past will repeat itself in a similar situation. Especially when a certain outcome did repeat itself myriad times, we tend to count on it doing so again, but there's no certainty that this next experience will give us a repeat performance—and when it doesn't, we feel cheated, confused, maybe stupid. Certainly we tend to feel overly responsible for "the failure."

But are we responsible for the fact that life is unpredictable, outcomes uncontrollable? Of course not. The only thing required of us is effort.

Cultivating New Behaviors

You Are Responsible Only for Making the Effort, Nothing More

I can practically hear some of you scoffing. When I was first introduced to this idea, I scoffed, too. How could I not be responsible for what might happen next in a plan that involved me, especially if I was the one who had set the plan in motion? That went against all my training! I know I'm not alone in this either. Most of us learn early to confuse effort with outcome. We learn that we must always finish what we start—and get good results! If we don't learn this in our family of origin, our bosses and workplaces will usually step in to teach us this lesson early on. We are praised for being extremely responsible and criticized for not being responsible enough. Is it any surprise that we become so outcome-oriented? Becoming able to discern the difference between making a responsible effort and taking responsibility for the outcome takes courage and an understanding of our limits and the role of God.

I first heard this idea that "it's the effort, not the outcome" in Twelve Step gatherings. I sensed immediately that I might find great relief in this approach to life, but I doubted that I could adhere to it. I had always been so results-oriented, and besides, maybe this worked in Twelve Step settings, but what about in the rest of my life? Wouldn't I continue to be judged based on outcomes, especially if an outcome was perceived as negative?

Yes, perhaps I would, but as I quickly learned, that's no excuse for perpetuating the illusion of control myself. Wherever we look, we will find people who continue to confuse effort with outcome. Any time we work with others on a project, they will tend to misperceive where our responsibility begins and ends. This offers us an opportunity to apply our little aphorism: The effort of any plan or action is ours, nothing more. The only thing we can rightly take responsibility for is our effort, and only for the part of the project that specifically needs to be done by us. And then we must take our hands off, regardless of what our coworkers or cohorts might be thinking or saying. This will not be easy—and it may well expose us to criticism—but it is the right thing to do.

Earlier in the book I made reference to "learning partners" or those people who travel by our side while at work or play, in the home or elsewhere, specifically because of the lessons we need to learn and teach one another. Our learning partners offer us an opportunity to share our perceptions of those situations that include both of us, with no expectation that our perception will be well received.

When we are working with a learning partner who has never operated according to the principle that we can only take responsibility for our effort, not the outcome, we come to see which part in an experience is ours and which part is God's. Our actions have the capacity to open coworkers' eyes, too. By only taking responsibility for our efforts, we make it possible for the other person to find a bit of relief and peace as well.

Don't Look Past Your Nose

By now you've undoubtedly heard and read, perhaps many times already, that we need to live strictly in the moment if we want happiness. But it continues to bear repeating. In fact each time we hear or read it, we are reminded to do it. And we all know this takes practice! Most of us are very good at being future dwellers. As children we planned for the day we would drive a car. As teenagers we planned for the day we'd go to college and/or marry. As soon as we joined the workforce, we planned on the first promotion and then the next one too. Looking ahead can have its positive side, of course. We do need to plan where we want to go in our lives, occupationally and personally, in order to seek the right preparation. The problem comes when we live in the future plan rather than in our current experience; in doing so we miss entirely what our life is teaching us on a daily basis.

At the same time that we can get so stuck in future plans, we also tend to be called by the past. In fact, as we were just discussing, we habitually rely on the past to interpret what is happening right now. But the instant we go to the past for edification about the present moment, we lose sight of the present moment. The present won't wait for us to notice it, to appreciate it, to learn from it, and to be grateful for it. It can't. It's gone in an instant, that very instant that we let our mind wander to another time and place.

No matter how clichéd it may have become, it is no less true: Being anywhere but here, now, absolutely denies us the peace we each deserve. When our minds slip backward or move into anticipation of the future, we lose out on the chance for inner peace and find ourselves in regret or fear. Even if our recollections or anticipations are joyful, we miss out on the very special and divinely selected experience that has been given to us right now and only right now. What will come our way a moment from now is something else entirely.

Let me remind you of my experience with my PhD dissertation committee member. Had I, in that moment, let any past failures or my incessant fear about the future take over my mind, I would not have been successful in our exchange. And I probably would not have received my degree, short of a total rewrite of the dissertation. And I would not have experienced the absolute presence of God, who I do believe is always waiting "to be noticed" in every single moment.

Somehow I knew to take that deep breath and trust in only that very moment.

We have only so many moments to live, and we have no guarantee beyond this one. No crystal ball can foretell how much time we have left. But if we wrap ourselves in the present moment, like a soft comforter, we will be at peace. We will be living in the very manner God wishes for us. The special gift of choosing this way to live is that we will never doubt God's will for our lives. Nor will we ever live in fear. Now is synonymous with peace. Should you have any doubt, wrap the comforter around you and test this hypothesis.

Stop Worrying about the Future

Most of us have heard too many tragic stories about friends who died quite unexpectedly, and I always wonder (perhaps you do, too) if they were having fun at the moment of passing. Were they living in the moment or busy worrying about an upcoming event, or fretting over the outcome of a situation already in motion?

Worry is a state of being that is only possible when we are not living in the present. It is evidence that we are anticipating a future that we think will mimic our past and the painful experiences that we don't want to repeat. We worry because we are uncertain of God's availability. Was he/she there in the past and we didn't listen to the guidance? We can be certain that God was there. But we may not have been; we may have been projecting into the future, as we are doing now.

Our minds can only hold one thought at a time. Do we entertain worry or the presence of God?

God is available right now. God will also be available in the future when we get there. What we must remember, however, is that God's presence can't be experienced except moment by moment, and that means we have to show up in each moment. Getting ahead of this moment in regard to our relationships, our vocations, our dreams, and aspirations simply prevents us from knowing God. When we commit to staying in each moment with God, we will have no fear; we will know, without question, that we have absolutely nothing to worry about.

If I sound pretty single-minded, it's because I am. My own experience has been a great teacher. In my role as mentor to a number of young women, I often say, "Don't get ahead of your nose." It's a great reminder that one is projecting, and it quickly brings us back to the present. I also suggest that whenever thoughts of the future come into your mind, you envision blowing them away. This may sound silly but it's effective. I have used it for years.

In my work as a writer and speaker, I often have a very full schedule. If I begin to think about every activity on my schedule, or even just one that is a few weeks away, I can get fearful and overwhelmed (both feelings quite unnecessary once I have done my research and outlined the talk). At that point, it's time to return to *now*. Whenever I let the future, rather than the present, call to me, I miss the peace of the moment. At these times, I try to follow the suggestion I've already mentioned: I blow my mind free of the thoughts, and I practice, once again, trusting that God will help me handle all that I have signed up to do, when the time to do it arrives.

In the Twelve Step rooms I frequent, one repeatedly hears the suggestion: Keep It Simple. These three words can change a life. If we stay in this moment, where God never fails to be, all the answers we seek will present themselves, and no worry will be able to hold us hostage.

Find the Joy Right Here, Right Now

How is this different from the ideas we've just been discussing? Here I want to stress that joy is of our making, and it is most easily made when we acknowledge God. I am inclined to say that acknowledging God is a necessary exercise. At least I have found it so. As I have said already, our minds can hold but a single thought. If God is that thought, every experience has the capacity to instill joy in us.

Of course I am aware that tragedies do occur, and none of us is immune to them. But if we allow God to handle whatever is happening and to comfort us at the same time, we will become aware that all experiences are orchestrated; they are fragments of a bigger picture, and the part each person plays is necessary.

I am not suggesting that God inflicts tragedy on us to teach us something. In fact, I don't believe that's ever the case. However, we have all observed that "bad things do happen to good people," and in those instances, if we turn to God for guidance, understanding, and acceptance of whatever has occurred, we will experience peace as well as joy, in time.

Joy is always available to us, moment by moment. But we must keep our minds open and pay attention. A closed mind or a mind filled with fear or judgment will never know joy. A red rose beginning to open, a willow tree swaying in the breeze, the rainbow after a shower, the dew glistening on each blade of grass in the early morning, a baby taking her first steps—all these moments hold the potential for joy. Every moment of every day we can see evidence of God everywhere. And we can feel overjoyed by this evidence if we want to. The decision is ours.

CHAPTER 4

Change Your Mind

—

Shifting our perspectives is a tool I was introduced to in *A Course in Miracles*. In fact, in the course, a miracle is defined as nothing more than a "shift in perception." Any number of thoughts we harbor on a daily basis are fleeting and not harmful in any way. Some, in fact, are positive and helpful to ourselves and others. The key lesson in this idea is to recognize our power to take charge of our thinking and, when we are not being helped by it, to be willing to change it.

The whole premise of this book is that if you don't like what you are thinking, particularly if it is harmful to you or others, you can change it! What a simple idea. But is it really possible? Indeed it is. And it doesn't mean living in a state of denial about "reality." It means only that we don't have to harbor any thought, bad or good. It is said that whatever thought we harbor is what we give power to, and it determines, with our "blessing," what kind of experiences we will have. I have certainly found that to be true. Read on.

Cultivating New Behaviors

Recognize that You Choose Your Thoughts

When I was first introduced to this idea, I simply couldn't appreciate its power. I was convinced that my thoughts were either "just there," floating in the atmosphere waiting for me to grab them, or that they were caused by the actions or opinions or words of someone else. I was surely not responsible for them. And even if I was responsible, so what! What is, is. Or so I assumed.

Living this irresponsibly for more than three decades, not being accountable for my own thoughts, allowed me to wallow in self-consciousness, insecurity, self-pity, and indecisiveness. It gave permission for my rage and for my conviction that I was always being treated unfairly. And it fed the ongoing fear that so held me hostage. By not exercising the power to change my thoughts, I was continuously sidestepping the lessons I would have learned and needed to learn through honest exchanges with other people.

The idea that I was responsible for my thoughts meant that I could no longer blame other people for what happened to me, and that idea was both frightening and humiliating. I would have to take responsibility for making my life different; I would no longer have my parents or husband or friends to blame. I would no longer have an excuse or an escape.

But once I got over the initial resistance, a resistance that was fueled by fears of new behavior, I began to see that this knowledge—that we choose our thoughts and always have, even those hideously mean-spirited ones—can be very empowering. For instance, it means that no one can put us down and hold us there. It means that no one can make us a failure at anything we try. It means that we are as smart as our willingness to do the footwork. It means that we can change any experience we might be having in the middle of it! All we have to do is change what is in our mind.

Our thoughts determine who we are, how we perceive ourselves physically, mentally, spiritually, and emotionally; how we perceive others; and how we plan for and experience our lives on a daily basis. Are we smart enough? Do we sense God as our companion? Do our fears rule our behavior?

Our thoughts also determine whether we view our companions in a positive or a negative way. What we recall of the past, a past that is gone, is often not helpful, even though some memories might be good ones. The next twenty-four hours will unfold as a reflection of our expectations, which of course are controlled by our thoughts. Living in the moment ultimately requires that we let the past be over.

Emmett Fox once famously said, in a slight twist on *Cogito, ergo sum*, "As you think, so you are." It's true. Our thoughts are everything. Nothing exists without our first thinking it. I would take Mr. Fox's idea one step further: "And if I don't like what I am, I need to be willing to change what I think."

By extension, then, I can only be what I think I am capable of being. But, and this is a very important but, I can develop in formerly unimaginable ways through making the effort to change the thoughts that have held me hostage. This is true for all of us. If I want a peaceful life, and I do, I know what I need to do. Do you?

If Your Thoughts Are Making You Unhappy, Change Them

Seldom do we understand, unless we have managed to educate ourselves through walking a spiritual path, that nothing is real but our thoughts, and they are creating whatever reality we are perceiving. And if we don't like our reality, we can change it. We tend to cling to our old thoughts because, no matter how much misery they may cause us, at least we always know what to expect. They lend security, albeit false security, to our lives. Or so we think. We have our preconceived notions about who is who and what is what, regardless of how wrong we might be.

The thoughts we are held hostage by were handed down to us by parents or educators or friends and other loved ones. They are not written in stone. The fact is, we can free ourselves from the past and from any thought that hasn't comforted us. When your thoughts no longer fit your reality, change them! You may have to keep working at it, keep challenging your thoughts and ensuring that they're not holding you hostage to some outdated picture of the world, but the choice is always yours. In every moment, we get to choose.

Believing Is Seeing

You know how it is said that different witnesses to an accident will remember decidedly different details—and not just the events, but the key players in them, too. Not surprisingly, people are often stunned to hear how someone else saw the same event. Deciphering an optical illusion goes much the same way. Look at the picture one way and you see one image. Cock your head slightly, and a different image emerges. Does this make one image the "real" one and the other image a mirage? Not really. Is one witness's view of an accident the correct one, while all the rest are wrong? Not necessarily. Only if the accident was filmed can the real truth be known.

The point here is that people are constantly editing what they see. The editing is generally unconscious and would most likely be denied if pointed out. But it happens nonetheless. What causes this editing process? Why can't we just see what is there to see? We have to look at more than the present moment of any experience to understand how these discrepancies occur.

As much as we may want to live in this moment only, we are generally prejudiced by what we have seen in the past and by what we want a particular experience to look like. And that prejudice colors how we see things.

Some might ask, is that necessarily a problem? Is change really necessary? My response is this: Your degree of peace should be the deciding factor. If you are content, there is no reason to seek change. If you are occasionally agitated, you may want to consider alternatives to the way you select what you think and choose to see. But if you are unhappy and ill at ease or often feel argumentative and unable to concentrate, you may want to seek another way of seeing the world around you. You may want to lay aside your judgments, for instance. Or you may want to devote a few moments to gratitude for the many blessings that have become evident in hindsight. Seeing the world from a more hopeful perspective can have a profound impact. Deciding to seek a more peaceful life for yourself benefits everyone else too. That's what is so exciting about our taking on this responsibility.

Shift Away from Negative Thoughts, Instantly

We live as though we can't help how we think. But we can. The negative thoughts we have were created by us; they are nurtured by us and can only be changed by us. There is only one thing standing in the way of making this change: ourselves.

There is a process for changing how we think. The first step is to be willing to give up a familiar pattern of thinking, and this is a step that many people stumble over. In fact, many of us don't even recognize that our thoughts are negative. We think they simply are. But once we become aware that a pattern is not working for us, the first step is to be willing to change it.

The second step is to envision yourself in new circumstances, fulfilling a new role perhaps, at work or at home or among friends. See yourself handling a challenge with ease that has baffled you in the past. See yourself the way you want to see yourself! Envision yourself in a detailed way.

Let me share an experience I had envisioning myself in a setting I was about to face. While I was preparing for my final oral exam for my PhD from the University of Minnesota, I happened upon an article in *Psychology Today*. In detail it explained an experiment that had been tried with skiers preparing for the Olympics. One group of skiers practiced on the slopes daily, as had been the custom of all of the skiers in past years. The other group envisioned themselves practicing, making sure to do all of the runs, seeing themselves successfully maneuvering the terrain throughout their race.

When the games actually occurred, those skiers who had merely envisioned themselves successfully competing scored better. The study concluded that when we see ourselves successfully accomplishing whatever our challenge is, we will be able to rely on that vision as the guide for a second success.

As the day of my exams drew nearer, I began envisioning myself at the table with all of the professors who sat on my committee. I watched each of them pose questions to me and I envisioned myself smiling as I responded successfully to their many queries. I did this practice in meditation for two weeks prior to my final oral. When the day came for me to sit with them at that table, I felt quite comfortable and confident that I could answer their questions; after all, I had already done so!

Painting this portrait of who you want to be can be a lot of fun. Try this yourself. Envisioning helps us grow into who we want to be.

One last reason for changing our negative thinking, and some would say the best reason of all, is that it will change how we treat everyone else in our lives. And treating others better changes more than just their lives. It ripples outward in infinite circles.

CHAPTER 5

Choose to Act Rather Than React

In 1971, I was teaching a personal writing class at the University of Minnesota. One of the books I asked the class to read was John Powell's *Why Am I Afraid To Tell You Who I Am?* Naturally I had studied the book before assigning it, and, on page 38 of the edition I was reading, Powell related a story that rocked my world, one that I recognized contained a profound lesson for me, even though I was not yet ready to apply it to my life.

Powell and a friend were strolling down a New York City street, a walk they took on many occasions. They stopped at a newspaper vendor's stand for the daily paper, the same stand where Powell's friend always stopped. The vendor was exceedingly rude in spite of the generous tip he received. After walking away, Powell simply had to ask his friend why he was so nice to a vendor who was rude virtually every day. He said, "Why should I let him decide what kind of day I am going to have?"

I was stunned by his response. It was my first inkling that I actually had a choice in how I reacted to others and that I could reinterpret, if I chose to, most of the experiences of my life. Since childhood, I had been watching the faces of other people for clues as to my worth, and in my family of origin, most of the faces were stern or not even looking in my direction. When I was being frowned at or when any of the words directed toward me seemed harsh—and many of them did—my confidence and self-esteem declined a little bit more. If I wasn't being directly spoken to, I often felt invisible because I sought eye contact and got so little.

For years I judged myself wholly based on the external stimuli I received. When I wasn't being showered with loving attention, and seldom was this the case, I felt deflated and often groveled. I am embarrassed to admit that I behaved like this for years. What I now gratefully know is that the behavior of no one, whether a parent, a friend, a husband, or a boss, can control how I feel about myself or how I act. It took me a long time to understand this, an even longer time to accept this as true, and more than a few years of hard work to fully embrace it; but it has given me a freedom I cherish and one I know I will never relinquish.

Cultivating New Behaviors

Stop Being So Dependent on the Opinions of Others

Many of us learned early to react to life and circumstances rather than to act on our own behalf. We learned to let other people's behavior determine how we were going to feel about ourselves. Making a conscious choice to act and not react takes forethought. It takes willingness to be more responsible for ourselves and a commitment to remaining independent of, not dependent on, the opinions of others to establish the sum and substance of who we are. For many of us this can be a huge step.

Our decision to take responsibility for who we are and what we will allow ourselves to feel and say in the midst of any encounter sets the stage for much healthier relationships. It will take some getting used to, and our partners might not like our new "independence" because it means they no longer have the capability to control our behavior, but in the long run getting out from under other people's control is a very good thing for all parties. Every time you practice this new behavior, you will have a sense of personal power that you didn't even know you were capable of.

Taking advantage of the numerous opportunities that crop up day to day to act rather than react to the ebb and flow of our lives relieves us of our dread of being around people who want to put us down or ignore us or who are just plain mean-spirited.

I don't want to suggest that learning how to act rather than react is only of use during difficult encounters. It's just as important to take charge of our behavior while interacting with people who are loving and supportive. The lesson to be learned here is that we are capable of determining how we actually want to respond in every situation, and then doing it!

Avoid the Knee-Jerk Reaction— It's Almost Always Wrong

This suggestion seems so pedestrian that I considered not including it. But my own experiences tell me that it's so important it shouldn't be overlooked.

In my family of origin, quick reactions were common and often angry. Unfortunately, my brother and I bore the brunt of many of them, and as a result, I had to retrain my instincts when it came to interacting with others. I realized early on that taking the time to respond thoughtfully would almost always serve me better than the quick reaction would. Our quick reactions, though not always wrong, are also not predictable. Sometimes they will be appropriate, but more often they will complicate the situation. Only in matters of imminent danger should you throw caution to the wind and react quickly. And even in those instances, the better choice is to be thoughtful and focused before taking action.

Okay, so how can we avoid the knee-jerk reaction? By taking a deep breath before doing anything. It sounds so simple, so obvious, and yet it's the approach that will work every time. Just take a single, deep breath and then watch your perspective change. You will feel less emotionally charged and become aware of an inner peace that had simply not been present before.

The combination of a new perspective, greater emotional clarity, and a sense of inner peace assures us of making a good decision, and this allows us to be of more consistent help in difficult or stressful situations. Another benefit of taking a good breath before responding is that deep breathing always reduces our stress level, which can be of tremendous long-term health benefit. Finally, and in my view most importantly, by responding "peacefully" to every circumstance we can, we make a contribution toward the peace and well-being of everyone present.

The peaceful response serves as a great example to others that they can also respond peacefully when their opportunities arise.

Detach from Other People's Business

Minding other people's business simply isn't the work we are here to do, regardless of how seductive the idea may be. We each must make our own journey, and even when it appears that someone we love is making a poor decision about an important matter, unless we are asked for advice, it's not our place to offer it. Besides, minding your own business will keep you as busy as you would ever need to be.

Detachment, perhaps a word unfamiliar to you in the context of relationships, is the only appropriate stance. If you are tempted to correct, control, or judge what another person does or is planning to do, detach. It is the loving thing to do. Even if you think the other person's plans are dangerous or foolhardy, it still is not your responsibility to try to change his/her mind.

How foreign this idea of detachment may seem. We think of getting entwined in the lives of others as being helpful and loving; we want to show them the right solution to a problem, or the method to use to resolve a conflict. We want to "save" them from the mistakes we have made, thus allowing them to bypass some of the heartache we experienced. Aren't we just showing compassion? What could be so wrong with that?

What's wrong is that we are preventing them from learning what they need to learn, from acting on their own behalf. We can only know the world as our eyes and minds and hearts experience it. We have to accept that the people around us are relying on their eyes, their minds, and their hearts to see the world they need to see in order to experience the lessons they are here to learn. Even if we, in fact, do understand their situation better than they do because of our objectivity, it's still not our right or responsibility to take charge of their actions. They have come here to do their own learning; we have come here for ours.

I can still recall the first time I heard that we "come here for specific lessons." It was very early in my recovery from addiction. I was new to the idea that each of us has a unique spiritual journey, unlike all others; that we meet whom we need to meet to learn what we need to learn. In fact, I was a bit spooked by the idea. All I could think about at first were the many close calls in my life, the many times I tempted death, and I couldn't see how those experiences possibly could have been purposeful. Fortunately I had a good friend who simply suggested that I not try to understand but instead lay aside my disbelief and act as if I agreed. She suggested that I begin by expressing my gratitude for every experience in my life, and that honoring all of the people in my life, past and present, as necessary "teachers" would allow me to see them in a new light. How right she was.

Gratitude for what was and what is, regardless of the circumstances, is a very powerful tool, and it can transform our lives and all of the lives we touch as well. Additionally, we must allow all those traveling this path at our side to experience their lessons without our interference and to cultivate their own gratitude if, collectively, we are to make the contributions we each have been selected to make.

Stop Looking for Someone to Blame— Including Yourself!

I can well remember my childhood refrain, "He made me do it." Whenever I did something punishable but wanted to avoid getting spanked, I would just foist the blame onto my younger brother. Seldom did it work, of course, which was lucky for my brother. But I was slow to learn that blaming others was more than just wrong; it was dishonest, disrespectful, and dehumanizing; most of all, it prevented me from achieving the growth I deserved and could only get through taking responsibility for my own actions.

Perhaps you have quit blaming others for your mishaps, but many among us haven't. The significant lesson, if you haven't mastered this yet, is that no one else is ever the cause of your behavior, and you are never the cause of anyone else's—no matter how inclined we are to pretend otherwise.

We live in a culture that consistently lays blame on others for the actions we take. Our country's many military entanglements through the years are prime examples of this. Some might say our country has no choice in matters like war, but on the contrary, there is always a choice, however difficult. Likewise, we justify our many individual battles by how we perceive someone else's actions. Our unwillingness to assume responsibility for who we are, for how we think and then behave, keeps us stuck, and the cycle continues. Nothing changes if nothing changes.

That's why it's so important to remember that you always have a choice, an opportunity to change yourself and, by so doing, to foster change in others by your example. Just consider that the very next time you interact with someone. Every interaction gives us an occasion to reveal or resist our willingness to be wholly responsible for ourselves. By choosing to take that responsibility, you will feel both a sense of freedom from expectation and from always having to behave in the same old way and an awareness of your personal power, not just over these circumstances but over all interpersonal situations to come.

Part of developing this new muscle means refusing to accept blame for others' behavior and relinquishing the habit of blaming them for yours. Believe me, this will transform your life. Make no mistake; it isn't easy. Old habits die hard. But you have the rest of your life to grow into the person you were scheduled to become. You need not be impatient with yourself. Or anyone else, for that matter.

As long as you are making progress—and you will know this by the level of freedom you feel in the company of others— you are certain to arrive at your predetermined destination. And your example will serve to show others who still prefer to play the blame game that there is another way to experience life, a way that fosters peace and cultivates gratitude.

Don't Let the Mood Swings of Others Determine How You Feel

Being raised by a rageful dad and a passive mother who was the quintessential martyr trained me very well to let the mood swings of others dictate my feelings. My dad uncompromisingly demanded that we all believe as he believed, share every one of his rigid opinions, and live according to his rules. I simply didn't know I had other choices.

That is, until I began to rebel. From the age of fourteen until the age of thirty-six, I was the rebel in our family, the one who fought the fights no one else dared to fight with my dad. During that phase I made numerous choices that were counter in every respect to the ones my dad would have made for me.

I am not particularly proud of this fact—there are better ways to assert oneself than through all that painful rebellion—but I share it because it illustrates so well how I willingly let another person's moods control my own moods and subsequent behaviors. What I suspect now is that my dad suffered from depression and, though not clearly alcoholic, he also displayed many of the symptoms common in the alcoholic family. His behavior was the result of his genes and training, as was mine.

This all may sound familiar. I referred to this syndrome of reacting to another person's behavior in an earlier chapter. But I bring it up again here because of the gravity of the condition. Children and adults are trapped by the mood swings of others, and whether they resort to rebelling as I did isn't the point. What happens to a person, and then a community, when behaviors are so easily controlled by the mood swings of others has dire consequences that in time affect multitudes of people. It's so important to remember that another person's mood reflects only that person, no one and nothing else. People who are frequently in bad or at least "distant" moods often bring out our fiercest desires to be liked, to be approved of, to be validated. It's easy to get sucked in. But we can't change another person's mood.

Period. And we should not even try. What we can do is change our behavior around those people. Or we can choose to stay away from them altogether so we won't be tempted to let their moodiness trigger an impulsive reaction rather than a thoughtful response.

It's up to us to determine our happiness. No one else is in charge. No one else is to blame. No one else gets the credit. Our happiness is tied to our willingness to be responsible for our own moods. That's a certainty—one of few in this life. It's also a certainty that any happiness we feel in the company of others is not the result of their attention, their happiness or good fortune, or their commitment to us. It's the result of our commitment to ourselves. Let's be grateful for that! Accepting this, accepting that we are responsible for ourselves and ourselves alone, is the key to allowing the rest of our lives to unfold as they were meant to do.

CHAPTER 6

Give Up Your Judgments

—

Essential to being part of the solution to a more peaceful world is a willingness to give up one's judgments. This calls on us all to change a deeply ingrained behavior. Most of us have grown so accustomed to our judgments that we often aren't even aware that we have them. Exacerbating this is the fact that we don't often recognize that we actually created whatever thought is in our minds. Thoughts so subtly emerge that we can pretend we have no ownership. But we are the owners and only we can discard them.

Giving up judgmental attitudes requires that we replace them with some other attitude. Our minds will not remain idle. The best attitude to cultivate and the one that changes everything and everyone—you and all of the people you formerly judged—is gratitude. Having an attitude of gratitude is what allows us to see everyone on our path as necessary and an opportunity for us to express unconditional love. You see, judgment and love cannot coexist, and we're expressing one or the other almost all the time. Seldom are we indifferent to our experiences, to the people we are sharing those experiences with, and to the set of expectations we have created around those experiences. Becoming more loving, attempting to develop the attitude of unconditional love, in fact, is the real assignment we have been given in this life. No one can do the work for us. No one can prevent us from doing the work. And everyone benefits every time any one of us makes even a tiny effort to grow in our willingness to love rather than judge.

Cultivating New Behaviors

Your Judgments Reflect Poorly on You

Our judgments of others reveal how we feel about ourselves. They are often quite subtle, and it's so easy to deny them because we think we couldn't possibly have those qualities that we see in others. They are never helpful because they prevent any expression of love. They heighten the feeling of separation from others, which illustrates the feeling of inferiority that drove us to judgment in the first place.

Judgments absolutely undermine every experience we have, whether at home, with friends, or with strangers. This may be difficult to comprehend, but judgment is always fear-based, and until we acknowledge the existence of that fear and understand its root, we will not likely get free of our judgments.

Fortunately, becoming spiritually centered, in communication with the God of our understanding, and aware of our oneness with others, automatically pulls us out of judgment, which arises only when we are not spiritually fit. Never at any other time. And so we must cultivate feelings of love and connection to keep judgment at bay.

When I embrace the practice of unconditional love—seldom an easy exercise, I might add—I am able to see how similar I am to those around me, and my habit of judgment lessens. Please note the word "habit." Judgment does become a habit, and so can unconditional love, though it is more difficult to perfect. A tool that has worked for me (when I remember to use it) is to express a statement of unconditional love out loud every time a judgmental thought crosses my mind. Try it next time you find yourself gripped by judgment. As soon as you catch it, state your unconditional love. It works.

Root Out Fear

Let's look more closely at this idea that fear is always behind our negative judgments. Why fear? Fear of what? Of coming up short. Fear develops from our incessant comparisons with others. We think everyone else is better than we are, "has it more together" than we do. And, out of our feelings of inadequacy, we consciously or unconsciously want to undermine them, their confidence, and their capabilities in any activity we share. We think that judging them, and in the process hopefully reducing their success, elevates us, at least in our own minds for a few brief moments. What an insidious, unhealthy, and spiritually bankrupt way to live! But looking around at our culture, and at other cultures, too, we can see just how common this way of seeing the world has become.

The solution for this and every instance of disharmony in our lives is the same. Seek to know better the God of our understanding, and do only what he/she would have us do. Remember that we are loved unconditionally, never judged, and we can pass on that which has been so freely given to us.

It can be quite exciting to practice unconditional love instead of judgment, if we choose to see it as an opportunity that will change us from the inside out and change everyone we touch as well. Once again, it's about changing our mind and watching our life change too!

Your Judgments Imprison You

It's easy to tell ourselves that we are not judging, we are merely observing. But most often this is just a lie. Our minds are quick to judge, and just as with any other thought, that which we focus on becomes magnified. When it's the failings of others or missed opportunities or cynicism or mean-spiritedness that we choose to focus on, these are the attitudes that are magnified, thus injuring all the people on our path and on their paths too.

Of course the reverse is likewise true. If we choose to see the good in others, which is abundantly there, we will help to increase it in them, in ourselves, and in our communities as well, widening the circle of good with every glimpse. The choice to see the good is always available to us. It's a mindset we can practice to the benefit of all.

Fortunately, we can feel the benefits of this shift immediately. We may need to remake the decision several times a day, but when we choose to see only the good in others, rather than focusing on what we interpret as their unfavorable qualities, we feel better about ourselves and increase our capacity for forgiveness, which fuels hope. Our level of confidence and well-being increases and our spirits are lifted, allowing us to feel more peaceful.

Some would say that seeing the good in others is fulfilling God's will since that is how all of us are seen by God. Whether this is consistent with your personal belief system isn't particularly relevant. What is relevant is the awareness that moods change when we respond positively to the people in our lives, rather than holding them down by our judgments, which can always be felt even if not seen. Simply put, judging narrows our world; dropping judgment expands it. One of the easiest ways to change our minds is to utilize the help of God, as we understand God. Maybe you have assumed, up to now, that some things can simply never change. On the contrary, anything we want to change will change if we go to the right source for help. But we must also have the willingness to seek another perspective and to do the work that is required to actually change. It can be done. I am living proof.

Your Judgments Hinder Your Relationships

As long as we sit in judgment of someone, we cannot experience peace. With each judgment we make, we hurt all our relationships. Perhaps this seems like a very strong statement. I mean it to be, so much so that it bears repeating. *What we do to one, we do to all.* While sitting in judgment, we can neither express the love of God, nor nurture the idea of peace—either in our own lives or in the lives of those people who are sharing our journey. Being imprisoned by our prejudicial thoughts restricts the natural flow of our lives just as surely as it impacts the lives of everyone around us.

If judgments are so harmful, why do we so ably and eagerly continue to judge? The easiest way to understand this, from my perspective, is to see our minds as split in half. On one side we have the ego, which according to some is an acronym for "edging God out." On the other side is God or Higher Power or the Source of all wisdom. Choose whatever name suits you. The point is that seeing our minds configured in this way simplifies the question of exactly whom I am listening to in any given moment. I am always listening to one voice, one part of my mind or the other. My ego's voice is loudest, and it is always going to set me apart from the people I see. It never, ever draws me peacefully and lovingly toward anyone.

The sense of separation we strengthen every time we make an unfair, unloving judgment is "the stuff" of wars, just as surely as it's the stuff of every simple little disagreement we have in our families or our communities. Every time we allow our thoughts to be guided by the ego rather than by the wisdom that is also available, we add to the disharmony of life, a disharmony that gets played out over and over until it imprisons all living beings.

What we do to one, we do to all, and they do likewise! This cycle will continue until we make a determined effort, one thought at a time, to change it. And each time we make a more peaceful, affirming choice, we play a significant part in changing the world. Powerful—and true.

Choose to Be Peaceful Rather Than Right

Let's dive a bit deeper into this concept. It's through our relationships that we grow, learning the lessons that we were born to learn. Caroline Myss, in her book *Sacred Contracts*, claims that prior to being born, each of us determined, in conjunction with other souls, what we wanted to learn, and within which experiences we would learn specific lessons. Whether or not you resonate with this idea, it can serve as an explanation for the many unexpected, oftentimes unwanted circumstances we find ourselves in. If we can cultivate the idea that everything we experience is by choice, albeit a choice we may not recall making, we will be more willing to meet it and absorb it. In time, we might even be grateful, I think.

Looking at our relationships as somehow "chosen" enables us to look at the meaning of their presence in our lives, rather than resisting that presence and judging the people involved. From this expanded perspective, we gain an expanded awareness of why we, and they, are here. Our lives are filled with such glorious mysteries, each one designed to our specifications. Were we to embrace this idea, even for a moment, we'd see the past in a new way and be willing to accept that the future will bless us as well.

Our desire to know peace, a desire I think we all share, can be fulfilled in only one way, through the experiences we have with others. If we'd consider doing what is necessary to heal one relationship, we would miraculously experience a lessening of tension in all relationships.

How might we do this?

The next time a disagreement begins to surface, make the choice to say nothing. Believe that being peaceful is of greater benefit than being right, and back off. Express only love and acceptance, regardless of what your ego mind wants you to express. Be kind whether you feel like being kind or not. Anything less is sure to exacerbate the disharmony that prevails.

Look at each relationship as if it's the only opportunity you'll ever have to act the way God wants you to act. This alone can change everything in your life in a positive way. I'm thinking of the expression: Life is short, eat dessert first. I'd say offering the love of God, the love that we have been given, to everyone we meet is dessert because it sweetens each moment. It also sweetens the path for those who are journeying with us. Our most important work is how we treat one another. Whether we are airline pilots, teachers, salesclerks, or firefighters, we really have only one task, and that's to express love, not judgment. It's a decision—one that we often resist, particularly when we are being met with anger, disrespect, disregard, or worse. But the opportunity to express only love will continue to present itself, and it will come in many, many forms, many of which will not look as if they are deserving of love.

That's the real challenge. To continue to express love when it seems least deserved.

As I have discovered many times over, any person you resist loving will reappear, perhaps not in the same "skin," but in the contents of his or her mind. Our most difficult relationships, the ones we judge so harshly, are our finest opportunities for growth. Isn't this an interesting conundrum? The truth is, you cannot escape the lessons of this life. After all, you requested them.

Stop Judging—For Your Own Sake!

Think about how you feel when you are criticizing someone. Ashamed? Embarrassed? Small-minded? Hopeful that no one else heard you? That's no good. An excellent way to avoid these feelings is to quickly review what you are about to say before you say it. If it leaves you with a yucky, uncomfortable feeling, don't say it!

Our criticisms always reflect how we feel about ourselves; they mask our fear that we don't measure up. The irony is that every time we sit in judgment of someone else, we strengthen the very feelings of inferiority that we are trying to escape or deny or project onto someone else. This behavior becomes a vicious cycle. We criticize, we feel ashamed, we criticize again in the hopes that undermining the other person will elevate us and give us some relief from our insecurities. Does it ever really work? Does it make us feel better about ourselves? No! So why do it?

If peace is what we are after, rest assured that it will never materialize, for us personally or for communities or countries either, as long as we keep filling our minds with judgments.

Every time we make a more loving choice on how to behave toward the people in our lives, we increase our self-respect, our self-worth, and our awareness of God's unconditional love, all of which advances our willingness to practice these new choices again. Each "practice session" makes a difference to at least two people: you and the recipient of the kinder, gentler you. Although every thought and suggestion in this book, including the choice of acting from love, not fear, has the potential of benefiting many people, the primary benefit for you and me, here and now, is that our own lives will get better. Honestly, isn't that the main reason for making any change?

CHAPTER 7

Remember That You Are Not in Control

Throughout this book, we have been talking about becoming responsible for ourselves and giving up the need to control others. But the obsession to control other people can be very strong. It gets played out with our children, our spouses, our friends, even our employees or bosses. In some cases the obsession is so compulsive that we can barely function. There are innumerable reasons for this, of course, and we will be looking at a number of them in this chapter, but one of the most prevalent, to be sure, is that we think our successful control of other people will keep them "attached" to us, actually in need of our presence in their lives, thus assuring us that we are loved. In this instance, our desire to control is actually a defense against feelings of insecurity and inadequacy. The irony is that often the more we try to control people, the less willing they are to remain in our life. Their desire for "escape" is directly related to our obsession with keeping them dependent on us.

Remember when I referred earlier to the split mind?

On one side of the mind is the ego; its voice generally screams at us to assume control of a situation and to retaliate by attacking another person through words or actions. On the other side of our mind is the quieter voice of our Higher Power, who is constantly assuring us that we are loved, that we have all that we need in our lives to be happy, and that we do not need the commitment or adoration or dependence of anyone to complete us. Any time we attempt to control another person, regardless of who she is or why we want to control her, we have tuned out our Higher Power.

Accepting our powerlessness over other people doesn't come without strong resistance, intense mental focus, near-constant practice of letting go, and unyielding willingness to understand that other people simply cannot be controlled! Our disbelief about our powerlessness is evident everywhere—in our dysfunctional homes, among disgruntled employees, within the power structure of every government around the world. Every war ever fought is strong evidence that people everywhere continue to believe they have the power to control others. However, one side seldom wins. More commonly, the vanquished simply give up.

If having a peaceful life is our goal, then we must give up unpeaceful behaviors. Making the decision to free all of those people in our lives from our misguided attempts to control them is a great first step.

Cultivating New Behaviors

Back Off

This one's pretty straightforward. In chapter one we talked about letting other people manage their own lives. But here let me say it another way: Butt out! Don't go where you are not wanted. Don't speak unless someone honestly asks you for your input. As we've noted, it's not easy to remain quiet when we see friends or other loved ones wandering down a path that's not conducive to what we consider their well-being, but stay quiet we must. Our "preaching" will not only go unheeded, it will most likely create a breakdown in the relationships that may be permanent, making us unavailable to friends or loved ones when they are finally ready to seek the advice of someone they respect, someone they think has more experience or more wisdom.

Letting other people make their own choices, which might well turn into mistakes, is good for the other people and for us. If they allow us to choose for them, and we make a choice that isn't beneficial, we become their excuse for failure. We become the unwitting scapegoat for whatever goes wrong in their life, a burden we surely don't want and one that's not beneficial to our own journey.

There is another upside to backing off from the affairs of others. You will have more time to devote to your own life. This is a significant gift—albeit one you may not initially appreciate as you continue to obsess over how someone else is living. But you will grow accustomed to watching others rather than steering them, and the benefit to all concerned will be greater wisdom for making future choices. Finally, each one of us must take responsibility for how we live, who we are, and where we are going. Only when we step up to the plate of accountability are we becoming all that we can become.

Attempt to Control and You Will Fail

Occasionally we get "lucky" and other people accept our efforts at control. When that happens it's easy to get the mistaken idea that we were able to control them and it was good. In reality, however, they were the ones in control of their own actions; they decided to follow our advice. We were still not in our control. There is no other explanation.

If others do change because of something we said or did, which sometimes happens, we feel validated and this val-idation boosts our self-confidence. Unfortunately, it also encourages us to repeat our behavior relentlessly. Face it. Others change only because they want to. Not because we want them to.

So why do we incessantly try to do the impossible? After years of observation, coupled with my own unyielding commitment to changing this behavior in myself, I have concluded that we attempt to control as a way of quelling the threat we feel when our companions have opinions or attitudes or behaviors that differ from our own. The greater the threat, the more we try to control. But what we discover when we give up trying to control everybody and everything is that we suddenly have the time and opportunity to learn and change and grow within ourselves, so that we can progress to the next level of spiritual awareness that awaits us.

A surprise benefit, too, is that by letting go, moving on, and living our own lives peacefully and with intention, we often inspire others to change in the very ways we want them to change. Ironic, isn't it?

A good friend of mine once said, "The more I force things, the tougher my life is." I couldn't agree more. Applying a stranglehold on anyone or anything does little more than wear out our arms and sap the strength we need to do whatever our work for the day should be. Accepting that we are not the center of the universe and definitely not the center of anyone else's life isn't easy. It helps if someone reminds us that we are just another bozo on the bus, and that there is no shame in that. In fact, it should come as a great relief to allow ourselves to accept the freedom of living one life, one day at a time, in the comfort of our bozo-ness.

Unburden Yourself

Controlling other people is also a way of avoiding our own goals. Our fear of failure can be sublimated as long as we are looking at others rather than ourselves. When we spend our lives following others through their trenches in hopes of eventually leading them, we have a ready excuse for not succeeding.

This may not seem to fit you or your circumstances, but ask yourself, how much have you achieved of your own goals? If you are not reaching your target, think about where you are putting all that good energy.

Giving up the burden of control, illusory though it is, not only allows you freedom but also allows the God of your understanding to do the work that belongs squarely in his/ her job description. Too many of us have been trying to carry God's burden for far too long. And the result has been disappointment, frustration, chaos, missed opportunities that would have benefited us, and, adding insult to injury, often being angrily attacked by those very people we thought we were helping.

Time to face facts. Trying to control anyone else is a losing battle. Thank goodness! If you don't yet understand this, you will, just as soon as you begin the practice of changing your mind whenever you find it focusing in on someone else's life. An excellent way of strengthening this practice is by saying the Serenity Prayer, and meaning it, every time your focus has wavered from your own life: God grant me the serenity to accept the things I cannot change, the courage to change the things I can, and the wisdom to know the difference.

Being powerless over others is one of the best gifts we have been given on this journey. Trust me. You will be grateful, in time.

You Chose This Journey; Now Deal with It

Every choice, every experience, every person in our lives is here for a reason. No one shows up by accident. We chose every person and interaction for the lessons they bring.

This may seem like an outlandish idea. I ask you to lay aside your disbelief for a time and review your past. Would you agree that people often "appear" in your life carrying a message that you later discover you really needed?

We are all teachers and students in each other's lives. From some teachers we learn tolerance. From others patience. Someone may learn what letting go means from us. In every interaction we are privileged to learn or teach something of value. We can disregard what is being offered, but trust me, the lesson will come again. It has to because it is our lesson.

Wisdom comes in many packages, from many directions, in many sizes and shapes. I well remember some of the early Twelve Step meetings I attended. I was prone to tune out some of the speakers, thinking that what they had to say didn't mirror my life and was of little significance to my recovery. My sponsor at the time was very wise. She said, "Everything you hear carries a message that could save your life some day. Listen up!" Shifting your perception to allow that everything you hear may one day save your life has the potential of changing every future experience you have. Adjusting to the belief that you are receiving what you came here to receive—thus meeting whom you need to meet, learning what you need to learn, growing in the way you need to grow—makes every minute of every day a gift.

These lessons aren't all going to be life-changing; often they're quite ordinary. It's important to realize this so that we don't discount any of our experiences. We must not discount the experiences of fellow travelers either. Our interactions are by design, even when we can't grasp their meaning in the midst of the experience. With this shift in perception, situations that are particularly troubling suddenly raise the question: What lesson am I resisting?

The best rule of thumb is to assume there is always something to learn, thus something to be grateful for, and that others are looking to us as teachers whether we or they are fully conscious of it or not.

Rejoice in the fact that the journey is why you are here. Nothing is coming your way that you are not prepared for or cannot handle, particularly if you go to your Higher Power for strength. You are exactly where you are supposed to be, right now and always, doing what needs to be done. And what is true for you is true for others, too. Let them do their own listening and make their own journey.

Your Efforts at Control Only Lead to Disharmony

We have come at this topic of control from many angles, but our discussion would not be complete without including the problem of disharmony in the mix. Every day we have literally hundreds of opportunities to let go of other people, their actions, their opinions, their hopes and dreams. It's especially hard to let go when we have a special connection to a person. It may even seem uncaring. But entering into the decision-making process of someone else, uninvited, spells disharmony, sometimes a disharmony so grievous that relationships are severed forever. For instance, trying to talk a child, a sibling, or a good friend into ending what we perceive as an unhealthy relationship is foolhardy. However, a prayer for them is well-spent energy.

It is simply not worth the risk to your relationships to insist that someone handle a situation the way you see it. Even if you don't push to that extreme, you may not escape harming the relationship.

Disharmony is what we create when we go where we are not wanted. Harmony is so much more pleasant, and it's just as easily created. It depends on our making wiser choices. Nothing more. We have to ask ourselves at every turn whether we want to be peaceful or agitated, whether we want to have harmonious relationships or tension, and then act accordingly. In other words, if we want harmony in our relationships, we have to let other people live their own lives.

Letting go, learning to live and let live, and praying for the edifying journey we each are here to make are tools that will promise us peace, which is the gift we deserve and our final lesson.

CHAPTER 8

Discover Your
Own Lessons

Earlier in this book, we looked at the idea that our lives, and the people in them, mirror the contents of our mind, down to the tiniest details. If we want our lives to be different in any respect, we have to change our thoughts. This is absolutely central to living a more peaceful life. The first step toward changing our thoughts is to acknowledge our power over them. Minds are not empty vessels that just fill up, willy-nilly. Whatever is there we put there! Whatever we "see" in others, or in the circumstances that are beckoning to us, is the direct result of our thinking—and these thoughts are handpicked.

There's really no such things as an "accurate" perception. Our perceptions are always affected by the way we filter information through our own past experiences, our own fears, our own insecurities, our own determination to control. I would go so far as to say that our minds will subjectively distort or misinterpret virtually every experience we have, and we will behave according to this distortion. It's not surprising that we often end up in conflict—unnecessary conflict.

You have no doubt read or heard that every time we point a finger at someone for a supposed infraction (and many of us participate in an ongoing blame game) three fingers are pointing back at us. In other words, we project onto others through our accusations that which we want to deny about ourselves, and our denial excuses us from taking responsibility for who we are. If we want to have a different experience, a more peaceful experience of life, we must be willing to exchange whatever our minds are protecting or hanging onto for thoughts of love, peace, acceptance, and gratitude.

Cultivating New Behaviors

Get a Life

Millions of people waste countless years having other people's lives on their minds. Al-Anon, the Twelve Step program for families and friends of alcoholics, has a saying that always makes me chuckle. "At the time of death, an Al-Anon member sees everyone else's life, rather than their own, pass before their eyes." A popular term for this widespread condition, a term familiar to many of us, is "codependency," which means always focusing on other people. We do this for one of two reasons. The first is that we depend wholly on the outside world—on others' reactions to us and on whatever might be happening at that time—for direction on what we should be thinking and for who we really are and how worthy we might be. When we allow ourselves to be controlled from the outside in this way, we fail completely to appreciate that we have autonomous, meaningful, and separate lives. We become blind to the idea that we might have any specific purpose of our own, let alone any worthwhile, independent thoughts. We allow our lives to revolve entirely around the opinions, the actions, the plans, and the whims of others. For many of us, this feels like security; under the guise of being connected and empathic and compassionate, we absolve ourselves of taking responsibility for our own lives. We also rob ourselves of the opportunity to do so.

You'll recall the anecdote I shared in an earlier chapter about John Powell's friend who refused to let the paper vendor's rudeness determine how he felt. His example is such a good one because it illustrates the capacity we all share to live healthy, self-governing lives uncontrolled by the behavior of others, lives not even mildly influenced by our fellow travelers when the influence is detrimental to our well-being. What Powell's friend was able to do offers us a great shorthand example for what every one of us can do. It requires little more than a change of mind about how we see ourselves in relationship to others. And then a lot of practice.

The second reason codependents focus on others will sound familiar. It's all about control. Codependents live their lives either feeling controlled by others or attempting to wrest control from those same others. In either case, being the controlee or the controller adds up to a life not well lived.

In this second scenario, our task is to "let go." If you are playing the control game, letting go can relieve you of a heavy burden and free you from near-constant frustration, a frustration that can last for years, particularly if your intent to control is unyielding. Letting go allows you to replace the futile and unhealthy thoughts that have filled your mind for so long with ones that allow you to expand in ways you might never have even considered. As long as we keep our minds wrapped around the lives of others, we simply cannot fulfill the purpose for which we are here. Your own life is waiting for you. Don't tarry!

With Someone Else on Your Mind, You Miss Your Own Lessons

Many of us come by our codependency through the various roles we play in our lives. Certainly parenting requires us to have our children on our minds for periods of time because they need and deserve guidance. But even as parents, we must recognize that constant focus on our children, living through them, trying to control them, isn't always healthy for them or us. When we focus on them at the expense of focusing any attention on ourselves, we fail to learn what we came here to learn. And we stop growing. All kinds of caregivers find themselves sublimating their own lives, but this is never a necessity. We can, instead, choose to see caring for someone else as an opportunity to create and maintain healthy boundaries, even while in the act of offering appropriate attention. Obviously we have to be vigilant, asking ourselves whether our impulse to take an action might be preventing the other person from doing things for herself. When we start doing for others what they need to do for themselves, we serve no one.

Of course there are numerous ways of having others on our minds. I have touched on only a few. But all too commonly, we can get trapped by our own insecurities and then become obsessed with the imagined or actual capabilities of those individuals we are comparing ourselves to. In the process, we relinquish all opportunities to take advantage of the lessons that might be surfacing in our own lives, lessons that become apparent in the myriad interactions that evolve with the people on our path. Let's not forget, no one is on our path inconsequentially.

This idea, that we are here in these bodies to learn lessons, really mystified me when I first began my spiritual journey. Frankly, I had no idea what "lessons" meant in this context. Slowly, as I became willing to listen to the wise voices that surrounded me, my confusion lifted. However, it still took me years to appreciate that every single moment of interaction with another person was an opportunity to learn a lesson, if I wanted to take advantage of it. Even then, it was still unfathomable to me, however, that this had always been the case, not just for me but for all of us.

Now I know that our lessons are constantly vying for our attention. They were vying for my attention during my childhood and in the conflicts with my dad. My first marriage was fraught with struggles that were in fact disguised lessons that I failed to embrace. Lessons were vying for my attention in graduate school and on my first job after graduation. They continue to beckon and I am just as capable of ignoring them now as I ever was. All I know is that an open mind, a mind uncluttered by thoughts of others, is required if we want to be good students of life.

We are all teachers or students in one another's lives—all the time. This doesn't mean that we are necessarily aware of what role we are playing at any given moment. Nor does it matter. The dance continues regardless. In the final analysis, the primary lessons for every one of us, however unexpectedly they show up, are to be willing to offer and receive love; to listen intently to the words of others; to remember that God is always speaking to us through our experiences with others, making each of them holy; and to be grateful for each moment, knowing that nothing is real but each moment as we live it.

You Can't Hear Your Inner Voice if Your Mind Is on Someone Else

How is this so different from the topic we were just discussing? In the previous section we were talking about the habit of letting other people be the objects of our attention and the contents of our minds. But the emphasis in this section is on the inner voice, and our inability to hear it when we are consumed by thoughts of others.

What I mean by inner voice is the voice of love and gratitude and hope. But that's not the voice many of us hear when we quiet our thoughts. No, we have to work at hearing that voice above the noise. When I was growing up and until I got into recovery, I heard many voices in my mind, but they were seldom loving voices. They were usually putting me down or second-guessing my every decision. They often mimicked the words of my dad or, as I got older, my first husband. They were just as likely to be reiterations of all the adverse messages I myself had created, with no one's help, over the years. They were definitely not affirming me, and I couldn't seem to escape them. So when I heard friends in recovery talk about the loving inner voice, I felt embarrassed and uninformed. I hated to admit that I didn't know this voice and wasn't even sure I had one.

What I eventually learned from friends, and with the help of *A Course in Miracles*, was that there are always two voices present in our minds. (Remember the split mind I referred to earlier?) One of them is quite loud and will always misdirect our thinking and our actions. It's the voice that keeps us stuck in old behaviors and feeds our fears, our anger, and constant discontent. The other voice, which is just as present but so much quieter, is ceaselessly conveying words of love and gratitude and hope and kindness. It is always directing us to look for the lessons in every moment, to unfailingly cherish each moment as the only opportunity we need to fulfill the will of God, and thus contribute to the peace of humankind.

It's this voice that comforts us. In the act of listening to it, we become willing to see the good in others and comfort them as well. This voice makes us whole and ready to embrace the lessons we know are waiting for us.

The challenge is to figure out how to circumvent the louder voice of fear and tune in to the softer, gentler voice of hope and love. Actually, it's not difficult to do, but it is the unfamiliar path and requires breaking old, well-honed habits. We only have to decide to listen to the gentler voice and we will. Let's celebrate that we can change how we respond to the people and the events in our lives. Let's celebrate that our minds are under our control, not the control of anyone else. Let's celebrate that the willingness to take responsibility for doing only what needs to be done by us is a tiny decision that we can make and remake every day. Let's celebrate the knowledge that we have now acquired that we can change our minds and our lives will follow!

Obsessing about Others Can Make You Sick

There are many reasons for anxiety and depression. Some people suffer from situational depression or anxiety as the result of a harrowing experience, perhaps the death of a loved one, or the anticipation of a major event they feel unprepared for. On occasion, medications are prescribed that help to alleviate these short-term conditions.

Chemical imbalances in the brain have also been determined to cause depression or anxiety. In these cases, the disorder might be permanent, thus requiring the long-term use of medication. Many people I have had the pleasure of knowing function quite well in all aspects of their lives since finding a medication that's effective for their specific condition.

The bottom line is that these forms of depression and/or anxiety are treatable. No one has to suffer.

But it is also true that our obsessions with other people's lives can make us depressed and anxious, and these obsessions can be interrupted by the simple act of changing our minds. Part of what causes this sort of depression is our obsessions about others, which prevent us from living in the moment and acting in our own best interests. We are not learning the lessons we need to learn.

We cannot become exhilarated and joyful and aware of our significance to the unfolding of the events around us when we remain stuck in other people's stuff. Depression can also be triggered when we constantly compare ourselves to others and find ourselves falling short. Rarely do we see ourselves as equal to the subjects of our comparisons and attentions. The ego doesn't want us to be peaceful within our relationships or even our casual associations. It wants us to feel bad, full of judgment, and willing to undermine or even attack others. Therefore, it sets us up to be "less than," and depression willingly obliges us.

As we noted earlier, there are times when we need to be very mindful of the activities or behaviors of others—our children, for example. But there is a difference, a big difference, between being mindful and being consumed by what someone else is doing. Our children may need our attention, but never our obsession. An ill or troubled spouse may need our loving attention, but again, not our obsession. Our jobs need our attention, but bringing them home with us is not healthy. We need to be refreshed on a daily basis, and obsessing about our tasks while not in the act of doing them tires us out.

Being tired out by our obsessions is very often the trigger for depression. One thing we can be certain of is that when the mind is compulsively focused on anyone else, rather than on the joys of one's own life, depression is never far behind.

There is one sure antidote to this sort of depression, and that is the willingness to live in this moment only and to develop gratitude for the hundreds of blessings in our lives. We cannot recognize these blessings if we succumb to the inclination to focus our minds on others. The good news is that the blessings will wait for us. When we are ready to return to them, they will be there. Choosing to be grateful rather than depressed seems like such an obvious choice; however, for those of us who so easily identify ourselves only in relationship to others, it is a huge choice and not one that's easily made. As I have said so many times already, our lives are to a great extent mapped out by our habits of mind. Committing to the cultivation of new habits requires willingness and vigilance. The payoff, however, is immense.

CHAPTER 9

Do No Harm

Never do harm to another? Seems so obvious. The trick here is to recognize the many ways we harm each other, particularly when no one gets physically hurt. Not making eye contact with the person you are talking to or being introduced to, not responding when asked a question that requires an answer, not including a newcomer in a conversation that he or she has attempted to join—these are all forms of harm. Discounting the suggestions a loved one might offer in regard to a shared undertaking, perhaps a remodeling project or planning the details of a long-awaited vacation, can be harmful to the relationship as well as to the spirit of the partner whose ideas are not being considered. And one of the most obvious and common forms of harm is simply not listening to a person who is trying to talk with you. Some would even say that being ignored can feel as hurtful as being hit.

Harm wears many cloaks. One thing is certain: Both the one doing the harm and the one being harmed often don't know it's happening. The victim may feel hurt by the encounter and not know why. But harm is done nonetheless.

Cultivating New Behaviors

Do No Verbal Harm

Are you attuned to how your comments may be affecting others, either while you are making them or after? Are you quick to reciprocate with an unkind remark when one has been made to you? Do you pay attention to how you feel after being rude to a friend or stranger? Have you ever chosen to be kind even when you were not being treated kindly?

Our answers to these questions are usually quite telling. Taking them one at a time, and honestly addressing them, will give you a thumbnail sketch of who you are in the world, which can then serve as a kind of blueprint for becoming who you would rather be.

If you want to change the tenor of your interactions you must become aware of the impact of your words. We may not intend our remarks to be hurtful. We may, in fact, think we are being more than civil, at times even loving, but the expressions on the faces of those who are listening tell the real story.

Change Your Mind and Your Life Will Follow

None of us is very skilled at hiding how someone else's words or actions affect us. If nothing else, our tearing eyes or down-turned mouth or turned-away face will usually reveal our true feelings. Becoming aware of these expressions in others will help us make better choices the next time we are in conversation—with anyone.

Most of us don't intend to be unkind, except when we are speaking with avowed adversaries. Our unkind comments usually result from not being as focused on the moment as we need to be; they come from thoughtlessness, not mean-spiritedness. They come about because of our inability to have our minds in two places at the same time.

The solution is to get focused. It's not rocket science. Make the decision, then follow it by practice. Using the simple rule of thumb that you will not say anything to someone that you wouldn't want said to you can make all the difference. Once again, let's think about John Powell and his journalist friend who bought the newspaper from the nasty vendor. John's friend chose to respond kindly even to a very unkind individual. He chose the peaceful response. We mistakenly think, on occasion, that striking back is what's called for. And it often feels more than justified. But the repercussions of striking back can be both uncertain and unnecessarily inconsiderate. Simply put, it never helps us to be unkind.

Every situation we are in is an opportunity to choose the high road in our interactions with others. When someone is unkind to us, we don't have to reciprocate in like manner. It is no more difficult to choose to respond from a place of love than it is to choose to be unkind. It's just a different choice. A choice that benefits everyone. When we're in conversation, we always have options: to listen attentively, to feign listening, to subtly ignore, or to quite overtly ignore (by walking out of the room, perhaps?). Doing anything less than giving our full attention is simply rude, and rudeness harms the spirit of everyone touched by the interaction. This can even be measured on a physiological level. A research organization called HeartMath studied the effects of unloving behavior on a person's physical condition. They then applied their findings in their work as consultants to Fortune 500 companies looking for more peaceful work environments. What they found is that not only the people we are unloving toward, but we ourselves, are affected mentally, emotionally, physically, and spiritually by our behavior. That's right. The health of every one of us relies on the "loving" behavior of all.

Why are we rude? Because we're distracted, we have our minds on other things? Yes, sometimes, but rudeness is often a sign of insecurity; it's a way of holding others at bay so they won't notice. It can be very effective but it's not favorable to any of the parties to it. It keeps people separate rather than joined in a common purpose. We will never find peace if we insist on maintaining our separateness. Conversely, there is no better way to be at peace than to seek a common connection. Let's face it. Verbal abuse is never, ever appropriate, even in the most antagonistic situations. It will never accomplish what the perpetrator hopes for, and it will always cause unnecessary injury to the psyche. The Dalai Lama is said to have once told a group he was appearing before that they had one assignment. It was to love one another. And if they could not love one another, they were at least to refrain from hurting one another. That's a pretty simple suggestion for living the more peaceful life. It begins with small positive changes that become habits. That's an assignment no one can fail if willingness is present.

Make a Daily Commitment

One of the central ideas of the Twelve Steps is that we must live one day at a time. Making this choice simplifies our lives and our decision-making in many respects, far more than we might at first imagine. I remember scoffing when I first heard this suggestion. How could I not be concerned about tomorrow, next week, or next year? If I didn't plan the future today, how would I ever get there? But when I decided to try it, I felt a great sense of freedom. The fact is, we do have only today. In fact we only have this next moment. This may seem elusive, but trying to live beyond this moment is not only a waste of mental energy, it's a waste of emotional energy. Doing no harm on a daily basis is one way of acting on this important principle. Why might we need to make this commitment to ourselves daily? Because it's so very easy to overlook our behavior and end up harming others in the process. It's too easy to diminish other people in our thoughtlessness.

We make judgments and put-downs. We set people up for failure, sometimes intentionally but often inadvertently. Our words, our facial expressions, our body language all send messages, and if we're careless, it's easy to seem dismissive or unkind. Harm comes in many forms, and the habit of diminishing the people in our lives in any number of ways, be they friends or strangers, is so ingrained that we have to be vigilant to refrain from doing it.

Making the decision to do no harm is far easier if we commit to it just for today. With practice this decision becomes easier and the payoff is immediate. We feel soothed and relaxed, physically and emotionally. We no longer have to guess at how we will react or be surprised by our own actions. Each day will have a flow, a rhythm that guarantees we will experience peace and a sense of well-being.

We receive so much from making this simple commitment, and yet, the pull to practice old behavior drags at our heels nearly every minute of the day. Not because we are intentionally mean or thoughtless. Most of us are simply scared. Scared that others are getting ahead of us—financially, professionally, maybe even spiritually and emotionally. Our fear pushes us to behave in a manner that harms everyone, including ourselves. In fact the injury to ourselves cuts deep, and the pain is not easily assuaged.

Every time we are harmed by our behavior, we more easily harm others at the next opportunity. And thus a vicious cycle begins right under our noses, and we sit by unaware—that is, until we commit to doing no harm each day. We can do this. We can choose, each day, to do no harm, and move to a whole new level of serenity. Isn't that what we're all after?

Refrain from Criticizing; It Is Never Loving

"I am just telling you this for your own good." How often have you heard that? Probably too often! Well, I have news for you. Criticism is never loving; it is never shared for someone's good. It is designed to undermine or create insecurities and doubt in the person to whom it is directed. So why do we do it? Because we don't feel good about ourselves. The irony is that our own discontent, the discontent that likely led to the criticism in the first place, usually escalates, which is just the opposite of what we had hoped for.

Holding another person down when we feel inadequate is extremely common and very debilitating. Booker T. Washington put it well, and simply, when he said, "You can't hold a man down without staying down with him." The insidious thing about criticism is that doing it once makes it easier to do it repeatedly. A day that starts out in criticism will usually become a day filled with criticisms, virtually guaranteeing a bad day for all involved. It is important to remember, too, that what we choose to criticize in others is nothing more than a reflection of ourselves. Our perceptions are our projections. We push our own imagined failings, however inconsequential, onto others because we don't appreciate our own humanity, our own frailties, and don't want to look at them. It is our lack of forgiveness for ourselves—over even the tiniest of errors—that propels us into being judge and jury of others.

Giving up criticism is like giving up any other bad habit. You make the decision to say nothing to your companions that is not loving. There is a Chinese proverb that delivers the message so well: "Don't use a hatchet to remove a fly from your friend's forehead." You make this a habit by repeating the decision to say nothing that is not loving each and every time your mind begins to formulate a criticism.

What about all the friendly suggestions (some might still call them criticisms) that are offered to us by friends or bosses who truly want to help us improve our approach to a particular task or game or way of thinking? It's easy to tell the difference between these and mean-spirited criticisms, isn't it? Furthermore, even sharing "helpful" ideas of this kind can be unwise. A better approach would be to ask if the other person might like some feedback, and if the answer is no, or if a response isn't forthcoming, to offer none. To quote Dick Cavett, "It takes a rare person to want to hear what he doesn't want to hear."

Once again, each and every encounter offers us a unique opportunity to make a positive difference in someone's life. Some would say that each interaction is holy. And God is always present. A great rule of thumb is to ask yourself, "Is what I am about to say going to please God, and if not, what might I say instead that would please God?" This has certainly guided me well. Our lives are passing so quickly, and in the turmoil of this world, we have little time to waste. Making any single moment more peaceful—by an action, a thought, a prayer, a memory—is worth the time we give it. Let's each make a difference to the people who share our space today. They will not pass this way again. Nor will we.

Do No Physical Harm

Physical abuse damages more than just the body; it damages the psyche, too. In fact what it does to the psyche is often even more damaging than what it does to the body. The physical scars will generally heal in time. But the memory survives.

Perhaps you have been the victim of physical abuse. You are certainly not alone. When you've been harmed physically, it can be so hard to let the past go. The ego is in charge of the past, and its survival relies on its success at keeping our minds filled with the awful details of every abusive experience. There is only one way to get released from its hold, and it's by turning our lives, in every respect, over to a power greater than ourselves and then breathing deeply. And then breathing deeply again.

A well-known actor who prefers to remain anonymous once said at an Alcoholics Anonymous convention that his life is none of his business. That simple statement is the key to living peacefully, whether or not our past is riddled with abuse. We can learn to accept what was and go on, if we allow our minds to be filled with gratitude for the present and the awareness that God is wherever we are, if we choose to acknowledge him/her.

This brings us to our own culpability as perpetrators of abuse. Desire to hurt someone else, particularly if you were hurt by that person in the past, might be understandable—but it's never, ever the right response because it keeps the cycle of abuse alive. Victimizing someone else is never appropriate, regardless of circumstances.

As with verbal abuse, physical abuse is the result of fear. It may not look like fear; in fact it may look like anything but. But it is. It takes great courage to walk away from a situation that cries for us to retaliate. But we must. Every moment, in every situation, with every person, we must focus on the peaceful response. That is the only way to healing.

Choose Always to Be Helpful, Never Hurtful

Every situation we find ourselves in, every single day, invites us to make a response. Our responses are not always audible or physical, but they are never really invisible. If nothing else, God takes note of them. Remember the Dalai Lama's suggestion to refrain from hurting anyone. That's just about the most loving and sensible and peace-promoting advice we might ever receive.

The decision to override the inclination to hurt others, regardless of their real or imagined violation of you, opens the door for any number of other responses. Go for the hurtful response, and your life contracts; allow other, helpful responses to surface, and your life expands. It's easiest to practice being helpful in the relationships we enjoy, but it's our more difficult relationships, the encounters that make us angry or retaliatory or depressed, that really educate us. These are the ones that can call upon all our strength and our courage for the helpful response.

What might being helpful actually look like? Must it always be time-consuming? Need it be costly? Does it require that we put aside our own needs? The answer to all of these questions is no. Being helpful can be as simple as listening to a person who needs to be heard, or smiling at a person who seems sad. Being helpful can be offering a simple prayer, only once or every day. It might be walking away from an impending conflict or "giving in" rather than insisting on being right. Practicing peacefulness is a helpful response, too. It helps all people present.

One of the best ways to be helpful is to use a gentle tone. Gentleness rather than rudeness goes a long way toward creating peace for everyone present, and even for those who will later, and perhaps unknowingly, be touched by the experience.

It's not difficult to be helpful. The only difficulty comes in making the decision to be. After that, it's just a matter of making the helpful choice, moment by moment, day by day.

No Action, Either Harmful or Helpful, Is without Effect

All our actions elicit reactions, whether obvious or subtle, positive or pained. That's why it's so important to be mindful of our behavior. All of us human beings are prone to acting thoughtlessly, generally because of our self-centeredness. We may not intend harm, but if harm is done, our intention is of no real consequence. That's why our vigilance is necessary.

If we could know for sure that committing a harmful act would have no consequences beyond those felt by our target, if we knew they would be "contained," so to speak, we might not need to be so concerned. Now don't misunderstand. It's never okay to act in hurtful ways. I'm just saying that if no one beyond "the victim" felt any repercussions, we'd be able to redress the harm we'd caused. But that isn't the case, and making reparations is complicated business and must not be ignored. Our actions always ripple outward, affecting not just the immediate parties involved but all humanity. We must never forget that.

That's why making every action helpful holds the potential for bringing about world peace. It all starts with our individual choices. This may seem arrogant or naïve, but think about it. Every kind act you or I make might trigger the willingness to be kind in another person. I'm reminded of the movie *Pay It Forward*. We are connected in spirit. When we help one person, not only do we help everyone everywhere, but we model a way of relating peacefully for everyone involved.

We learn by imitation. We have always learned by imitation. Those of us who grew up in families that were prone to hurting one another tended to learn dysfunctional behaviors as a result, but old patterns can be changed. New habits can be honed. Practice is the key. Spending just one day, even one hour, monitoring what is going on in our minds and then changing it if our thinking is not beneficial—to ourselves or others—would let us see a different world. We would be able, if even for a few moments, to envision a loving world and then take the actions that would best further it. Making a peaceful world is not someone else's job. It's the job each one of us is here to do. One moment, one thought, one action at a time.

Give Up Arguing, One Argument at a Time

Why do we argue? Why do we get into conflict? To cover up our fear. That may sound like too much of a generalization, but it's true. Consider the last argument you were in. More than likely you felt vulnerable or bullied or at the mercy of someone else's whims. And you reacted. You stood up to your adversary's attempt to control your behavior or your opinions or your future plans out of fear of where his or her control might lead you. And why was your adversary attempting to control you? Also out of fear. Arguments are always about two parties (or more) who are afraid, but most of us don't even realize that, let alone admit it.

When it comes right down to it, we all operate out of two emotions: love and fear. Fear, which is so prevalent these days, takes its toll on us emotionally, physically, and spiritually. And all the bickering that flows from our fear has far-reaching consequences. If we are in a constant state of agitation, we are not able to be present to the real lessons we are here to learn. Not to mention that the feelings of agitation that always linger long after the precipitating event keep us stuck in the past and unable to take notice of the lessons beckoning to us in the present. As always, our behavior in one situation spills over and, given enough practice, becomes a habit—in this case the terribly destructive fear habit.

Fear wears many masks. Silence. Sullenness. Tears. A verbal outburst. On occasion fear strikes out physically. Fear never helps any encounter. It always exacerbates the tension. Its hold on us can be merciless. The only way to become free of our fear and available for the present moment is first to understand why our fears are so powerful.

For the first three decades of my life, I experienced nearly constant fear. My domineering dad couldn't control me, my beliefs, or my behavior, and it made him crazy with rage. I was only too eager to react with a bit of my own rage. We argued all the time. I know now that our arguments were the result of our fears, his fears for my safety and my fears that I would someday be like him. What irony.

I would probably still be a woman filled with fear if I had not become willing to walk a spiritual path. My transformation didn't happen overnight, but just knowing that other people had learned to let go of their fear gave me hope. I am embarrassed to admit it, but for many years on this path I was still quick to argue. I haven't completely given up this behavior even now, more than thirty years later. But I am more willing, on a daily basis, to take responsibility for my part in an argument and then admit, to myself at least, that fear was the instigator.

I called this section "give up arguing, one argument at a time" for a reason. It's so much easier to change a behavior, an attitude, an idea when we narrow our focus. Promising to give up arguing forever, starting right now, opens the door to failure. How much better to say, "For this moment, this hour only, I will not argue." Then, when you find yourself on the verge of reacting to someone else's opinion or accusation or dismissal, you can assess what your own fear is about and relinquish it to the caring hands of your Higher Power. Remember, one argument at a time.

We do not have to remain in the clutches of fear. It has only the hold over us that we allow it to have. We always have the choice to feel love rather than fear. It's not mysterious. I have done it. All it takes is a willingness to change how you see a situation and the people present; to realize, as the need calls for it, that others' fear-filled lives keep them from being able to respond to life with love. But that doesn't prevent you from doing so. By choosing love, moment by moment, we change and we change those around us. This is a certainty. You can simply decide to give up arguing, one argument at a time. When an argument calls to you, look away. Say a prayer. Be grateful for your awareness that there is another way to see your experiences.

Let's be willing to prove that Margaret Mead was right when she said so long ago that the world changes one person, one act, at a time and only in that way. By giving up arguing, you become a change agent. Every time you walk away from an invitation to argue, you show others that walking away is a possibility for them too. This is how our actions ripple outward. Love or fear? The choice is yours.

CHAPTER 10

Quiet Your Mind

———

Our minds chatter constantly. Are you conscious of the chatter in your mind? For the next few minutes, pay attention to it. Maybe you are making a grocery or other "to do" list. Perhaps you are passing judgment on the person who just walked past you at the mall, and comparing how you measure up to her. Now your mind is wandering to how you have never been good enough or smart enough or pretty enough.

What about the driver who just passed you on the shoulder of a busy highway or the woman who cut in front of you? What thoughts are you harboring about them, thoughts that are drawing your attention away from the heavy traffic all around you? Are you wondering what your spouse might be planning for your upcoming anniversary? Or maybe you are thinking about the possibility of losing your partner—to another partner or to death?

Maybe your mind is on the sunny weather, and you are thinking about how good the sunshine will be for the flowers you recently planted. My thoughts often go, especially when I'm busy writing, to the dust bunnies that are everywhere in my house.

Our chattering minds can drive us to distraction! They're busy flitting from one scenario to the next nearly all the time. But it doesn't have to be that way. We can take control of our minds. We can enjoy peace, experience serenity, and become aware of the messages God has for us. We can, as the title of this book claims, change our minds, and our lives will follow.

Cultivating New Behaviors

Any Thought Can Be Released

Having thoughts is no crime, of course, it's just that our thoughts so often pull us off course. We put ourselves down; we judge others; we replay the past; we worry about the future. It doesn't have to be that way. We are fully responsible for our thoughts and can take charge of them whenever we need or want to. Isn't that empowering? No one can ever take away your identity. No one can take charge of your thoughts, and thus your life, without your compliance. No one can force you into positions that are not to your advantage. No one can foist opinions or attitudes on you. You are as happy or as serene or as peaceful or as self-assured as you decide to be. Whoever you think you are, you are. And any thought that doesn't nurture you in a positive way can be discarded, right now.

Sound too easy? Try it. Just one time, try it. Here is how to do it: When a negative thought begins to move through your mind, envision yourself blowing it away or shaking it out of your head. When a mindless, busy-making thought takes up space in your mind, blow it away, too.

This may sound silly and not very therapeutic or sophisticated, but it works! And personally I think that's what matters. I don't subscribe to the idea that every thought we harbor needs to be analyzed for its hidden meaning. Doesn't it make more sense to use whatever means you have for dispelling thoughts that are not making you happy?

It's rather like cultivating the ground prior to planting seeds to grow corn. We have to remove the weeds and discard the rocks in the soil before digging the furrows for the seeds. What we drop in the ground, what we cultivate in our minds, is what grows. It's not rocket science. Now try it. Blow away those negative thoughts. Now do it again. And again.

Choose Your Thoughts Wisely

We choose our thoughts. We choose to acquiesce to the feedback we receive from others, feedback that may not serve us well; we choose to remain stuck on past hurts; we choose to worry about the future. This is cause for rejoicing! If we can choose these unhelpful thoughts, we can also choose helpful ones. You are in the driver's seat. You will only be as content and peaceful as you change your mind to be. Nothing is keeping you from making this change, starting right now.

If a Thought Is Troubling You, Choose Another

How many minutes of each day do you spend feeling out of sorts or blue, perhaps angry and fearful? You don't have to. Whatever the feeling is, it has a thought behind it—a thought you can choose to change. Anytime. All you need to do is shift your perspective.

In *A Course in Miracles*, the spiritual pathway that I mentioned earlier, shifting one's perspective is referred to as the miracle. It is an action step, even though it's very quiet and generally very subtle. It requires a willingness to quit nursing whatever thought is behind the feeling that's negatively affecting your well-being, then inviting your Higher Power to choose a better thought to replace it. This is a refreshing way to look at our lives, I think. It encourages us to rely on the partnership we have with a Higher Power, if we choose to acknowledge that partnership, and it frees us from having to handle this shift alone.

Making just the slightest shift in how you see whatever is going on around you can change your inner dialogue entirely, thereby changing the thought and the feeling. All you ever have to say is, "God help me to see this another way." It may not seem that a new thought comes right away, but it does. However, our ego is cunning, baffling, and powerful, and it may pounce on the new thought, brushing it aside, before you even have a chance to embrace it, which only means you will have to repeat the process. Asking to experience the shift again is all you have to do. Practice, practice, practice.

The sense of empowerment that comes from being willing to seek a shift in perspective is profound. It means you don't ever have to be at the mercy of a feeling or a thought that you don't want. You also strengthen your partnership with your Higher Power every time you humble yourself enough to ask for help. The strengthening of your ties to God, however you define God, will serve you in so many ways. The more you make a habit of turning to that source for guidance, the fewer struggles you will have in any area of your life.

We cannot change the world because it is not our job, but we can change ourselves because it is. That's the most profound shift in our thinking we ever really need to make. God will keep reminding us of this and helping us do it. Or we can make it such an ingrained habit that we are freed up to give other problems to God for solving.

You Can't Hear Your Inner Guide without a Quiet Mind

Remember how I said there are always two voices in our mind—one that belongs to the ego and generally clamors for our attention and another that is gentle and quiet and can't be heard at all when we allow the ego to shout at us? The quiet voice wants to offer us spiritual guidance, solace when it's needed, and peace, but getting quiet enough to hear this voice requires us to wrest control of our minds from the ego. The reward for doing this is huge. Not only do we sense immediate relief from the chatter, which is nothing more than constant badgering by the ego, but we begin receiving spiritual guidance that will benefit not only us but our many companions as well.

Our lives are purposeful. This statement is applicable to every person alive. And there is only one sure way of knowing that purpose, and that's by making sure we are privy to the guidance we need. That guidance rests within each one of us, but it won't force itself on us. We have to be ready and willing and full of desire. Until we reach this level of readiness, we will not know peace. Until this time of readiness, the chattering voice of the ego will continue to disrupt our lives and our peace of mind.

Early in my recovery I was overwhelmed with anxiety about everything. I didn't feel confident about leaving my apartment. I was afraid to go to work. I didn't want my friends to know how scared I felt because I was ashamed of my feelings. I didn't want to look like a failure. We all had the same Twelve Steps to guide us, and they seemed to be doing fine. What was the matter with me?

Fortunately a friend left a book at my house that, in my fearfulness, I picked up. The book was *Illusions* by Richard Bach. I read it and loved its hopefulness, but what really made the difference in my life at that moment was his message on the back cover. "If you are reading this, you are still alive, which means you have yet to fulfill your purpose." This simple message was all the guidance I needed at that moment, and I felt certain that it was a message from my Higher Power, the same kind of message we are able to receive when we quiet our minds. If you can stay tuned to the calm, gentle voice inside you that truly cares about you, you will never have reason to doubt any decision you make. If you go to the right source for sustenance, guidance, comfort, and peace, you will not falter. If the message still seems a bit muffled because the ego is kicking up a fuss, just remember this: you will never fail to fulfill your purpose if you express only love to every person on your path. That's right. When in doubt, do nothing more than offer love or kindness or comfort to whoever stands before you. Whatever guidance you are seeking will be revealed in the midst of your act of kindness. And if you still feel uncertain, you will have added to the peace of the world nonetheless.

Change Your Mind and Your Life Will Follow

CHAPTER 11

Every Encounter Is a Holy Encounter— Respond Accordingly

—

One of the most significant changes of mind I have ever made was the decision to see every encounter as a holy encounter. Yes, whether embracing a family member or checking out at the grocery store, we are engaging in a holy encounter. Even our most mundane interactions are sacred, each one contributing a necessary thread to the tapestry that is becoming our life. And none is more significant than another. I have learned the lesson well over the course of my life: No one wanders our way by accident. We don't have to understand why they have come, nor do we need to understand what they may be seeking from us. Our one and only assignment is to respond to every person who crosses our path as a holy companion—and one who is likewise on assignment.

We are all interconnected. I actually find this a very comforting thought. It makes it easier to navigate through life. It takes the guesswork out of selecting how to respond to any given situation. All we need to remember is that if we are considering a response that wouldn't please God, we should reconsider. Silence is the better choice. Or taking the extra moment to reframe our response. Choosing to see every one of our companions—those we know well and those who are simply passing by—from the same loving perspective from which God sees each one of them, means we will never fail to respond appropriately. It takes practice, but even if we only remembered for an hour every day that every encounter has been orchestrated by God, we'd be far more likely to monitor our actions and make them kind, make them a reflection of the love God has shown each one of us.

Every time we choose to separate from our companions through judgment, we unnecessarily complicate our lives. It's really as simple as that.

Cultivating New Behaviors

No Experience Is Accidental

From very early in life, we learn to categorize our experiences as good or bad, educational or foolhardy, spiritual, accidental, tragic, lucky. It's very tempting to do so because that way we don't have to acknowledge that every experience is both holy and specific to what we need on our journey. Remember what Caroline Myss said about how we are each here to fulfill the contracts we have chosen to experience during this lifetime? This means that not one relationship or experience was or is accidental. It also means that elevating some while devaluing others misses the point.

By accepting this idea we begin to see that our whole lives make sense. They have a pattern to them; things happened—and continue to happen—for a reason. We no longer have to hang on to the hurt or anger or self-pity or confusion over the past that has fueled our negative attitudes. We don't have to let our memories of difficult past experiences determine how we feel. We don't have to blame anyone anymore for the hurtful experiences we shared. We can see that these experiences and people were preselected for this journey and, in so doing, choose to let go of all resentments. The freedom this offers is immense.

I remember hearing, early in my spiritual recovery, that we should thank God for every experience we have, while we are having it; that we need to look for the good in every one of our experiences. I was not easily convinced. I had had too many painful times in my life to believe it was all intentional and all holy. It took more than a little willingness for me to review my past with an eye toward seeing and then accepting that all of my experiences were holy, even the most painful, and that all were necessary to help create who I had become, and thus had been a blessing. Letting in the idea that there are no accidents allows us to give up our confusion, our fear, our spiteful anticipation, our preconceived resentments, our resistance, and our near-constant concern over outcomes. We can choose to believe that every experience is on its own schedule and that showing up for it is our only real job.

If this seems too simple or far-fetched, consider this: If you find out at the time of death that this way of seeing was all wrong, will it matter? I think not. In the meantime, it will have allowed you to be far more peaceful going forward.

Try to Find the Lesson in Every Experience

In chapter seven, I shared the idea that our lessons are repeated until we learn them. These lessons come to us through our experiences, which is why we should never discount any experience as unimportant. The experiences that deliver some of our most important lessons in this life may in themselves seem very insignificant—for instance, opening the door for an elderly man or woman and then gathering up their gratitude, which reaffirms how necessary is our expression of love and attention—but that doesn't mean that they aren't all part of the design for our lives. It is

Change Your Mind and Your Life Will Follow

our good fortune that opportunities to offer only love as the key lesson in everyone's life present themselves again and again until we fully claim them.

These lessons—which often come in the form of interpersonal confrontations that allow us to choose love over fear, acceptance over resistance, forgiveness over resentment—give direction to our lives. They create and sustain the relationships we have with others, both the ones we love and the ones we struggle in. They allow us to fulfill the purpose for which we are here and to bring about a change in the lives of all. Our interconnectedness means that a lesson mastered by one person is making its mark on others of us too.

One of the lessons I had to be given over and over through experience was that how other people responded to me was not what gave my life its meaning. I had to learn that the behavior of others reflected how they saw themselves, thus how they felt about themselves. Their behavior seldom if ever had any real connection to what I did or said.

This was a huge lesson for me because throughout my childhood and well into my adult years, I was nothing if not the mirror of how I perceived others treating me. I have elaborated on this idea already in other sections, but I repeat it here because finally learning the lesson I needed to master changed my life. And it changed how I treated the other people in my life. I really didn't know who I was until I took ownership of myself. And nothing about my life has remained the same since then. There are lessons in all our experiences, every day, big and small. As we begin to see what they were and are, we become more open and less resistant to what might be coming next. When we realize that what has already come our way was intentional, meant for our edification and spiritual growth, and necessary for us to fulfill our purpose, we naturally lose our fear over what is to come.

And that is freedom.

Everyone We Meet Is Destined to Be on Our Journey

We've discussed the idea that we come into this life having made sacred contracts with others, contracts for experiences that would benefit our mutual evolution. And here we are at this idea again. It is extremely important that we see the significance of each person as she or he passes through our lives. It is not by coincidence that they have come.

Holding the idea that each person and encounter is significant has the effect of heightening the joy of the happy encounters and lessening the sting of those that didn't seem to benefit us at the time. It alleviates the pain and confusion we sometimes feel.

I think it is safe to say that no one actually has any recollection of the contracts we made before we were born. And it's our forgetfulness that allows our fears to overwhelm us when we are in situations that seem painful or too difficult or confusing to handle. If we could even occasionally remember that we are exactly where we are meant to be, with the people we are meant to have an experience with, and with God as our constant companion, we'd feel so much more at peace.

Some of you might be uncomfortable accepting the idea that every one of our experiences is preselected, particularly if you have experienced physical or sexual abuse. To you I say this: If this is an idea that distresses you in any way, let it go. There is a popular saying: Take what you like and leave the rest. That certainly applies here as well. I just know that choosing to believe that the God of our understanding will never leave our side, and has never left our side, no matter what experience has befallen us, can be of tremendous comfort. It was never part of the plan for us to experience anything alone. And whether we choose to be joyful that our lives are following the path they are meant to be on or choose to resist the journey, we will still end up where we are meant to be. I just think getting there the more peaceful way makes the best sense.

Be Grateful for Every Experience

Another choice that we often neglect is the choice to be grateful. We ought to be grateful for every experience we have, for all of them, painful and pleasant, are important to our life's journey. But many of us fail to realize that gratitude is a choice, and a choice we have available to us all the time. The beauty of believing that gratitude is a decision is that it gives us the power to change our perspective on every circumstance in our lives. Of course it's easy to be grateful for the "good" stuff—our health, meeting our life partner, the birth of children and grandchildren. But what about the difficult or painful or confusing times? By becoming willing to be grateful for these experiences, too, we have the chance to learn whatever we need to learn from the experience. As I've said so many times before, even when it seems the most impossible to believe, it's still true that what comes to us is right for us—always.

Just think about your own past, particularly about those experiences that seemed really tragic or accidental but turned out to be important turning points or life lessons. You see, the whole picture is rarely revealed all at once.

Many say we couldn't handle the whole picture it if it were revealed, and that God gives us only what we can handle, a little at a time. I'm certainly inclined to believe this. For instance, had I known before my first marriage where it would eventually lead and why, I'd have been immobilized. But I survived the emotional upheaval when it finally came, and being on the other side of it now, with all of the gifts that have come to me in its wake, makes me very grateful for each and every deeply troubling situation that occurred. Every one of them was necessary for my development.

Making the decision to be grateful means letting go of doubt. Doubt is a waste of our energy. We don't have to like every experience. In fact, we can even sidestep an experience now and then, but if it's one we really need for our specific journey, I can guarantee it will come calling at another time. Our ego minds truly don't know what's best for us. Our Higher

Power does and we can be certain that no experience we need will be overlooked.

I find tremendous comfort in choosing to be grateful for everything as it is happening, even when I don't understand it or I am angry or hurt or saddened by it.

Once I realized that I would never have peace until I took myself out of the business of second-guessing God's infinite wisdom, I found the peace I'd been looking for all along.

Okay, you say, that's all well and good, but how does one cultivate gratitude? One excellent way is to make a gratitude list each night before you go to sleep. As this becomes your habit, you will find yourself far less troubled. You will know a peace you had not thought possible.

Through Our Relationships with Others, We Heal Our Minds

The truth is, we cannot heal our hearts or our minds in isolation from one another. Healing comes through relationship, through becoming aware of our great interconnectedness with everything and everyone else and our gratitude for that awareness. In isolation, we can pretend many things but seldom can we create a healthy self-image, or the inspiration to accomplish meaningful work. Once we relinquish the illusion of our separation and isolation, we become able to set and accomplish goals that may have seemed utterly unattainable in the past. We become willing to love and forgive, regardless of the circumstances in our lives. We come to see ourselves in one another and accept the frailties and short-comings of us all, while celebrating our strengths, knowing we share those too. These are the gifts of a healed mind.

Although Thomas Edison is an example of one person who often spent day and night alone in his laboratory discovering and fulfilling his purpose, most of us fail to discover our purpose for being alive when we're in a state of isolation. More commonly, our experiences with our fellow travelers give us the clues we need to discern why we are here. The work we are being called to do generally cannot be accomplished while hiding away from the external world.

In fact, we can never know who we really are unless we have others to interact with. Perhaps most difficult to understand, in all this, is that the people with whom we have the most difficult relationships are the ones from whom we learn the most. It is in these more fraught interactions that our minds are healed the most.

That's why it's so important to choose to be grateful for every relationship. We simply cannot know what God has intended for each of them to mean in our lives. We can only be sure that they are present to help us heal. The opportunities for healing our minds surround us.

We can ignore these opportunities by refusing to interact in a loving way with whoever is present on our path, but we really can't escape this fact. That's why it just makes good sense to choose the peaceful response.

CHAPTER 12

There Are Two Voices in Your Mind— One Is Always Wrong

The core concept of this chapter comes from *A Course in Miracles*, which, as I explained earlier, is a spiritual program that has as its primary focus a more peaceful life. According to the "course," there are two voices in our minds. One belongs to the ego, the other to the Holy Spirit (you may call this peaceful inner messenger your Higher Power or Great Spirit or Universal Source or whatever name you choose). Both voices are always available to us, but one is very loud and generally gets our attention. I am guessing you can figure out which one that is. The course tells us that the ego's voice is not only the loudest, its message is always wrong. So why do we listen so intently to it?

It is a mystery, really. The ego is not our friend. It will mimic a friend, but a friend it is not. It will attempt to make us feel special by setting us apart from others. It will speak to us of our superiority one moment and our inferiority the next, as a way of keeping us off balance and confused. Its very survival relies on our listening to it and only it; therefore, it will go to any length to maintain its hold on us. It always persuades us to give up our good judgment and wisdom and to face life from a position of anger or fear or aggressive behavior or isolation. The other, softer voice speaks to us of love and peace, surrender and forgiveness, hope and acceptance. It never draws a distinction between us and others. It always emphasizes our sacred necessity to one another. It will coach us into having successful and loving relationships. It will constantly remind us that we are always where we need to be and that the hand of God is always present.

Fortunately we all have free will, and free will allows us to choose the voice we want to listen to. We can always choose to listen to the soft, gentle voice of peace. We can choose to change our minds, and our lives will follow.

Cultivating New Behaviors

Be Vigilant about Your Choices

If what you are seeking is peace, you must be vigilant about the choices you make. The ego will often beckon you to choose gossip, criticism, comparisons, judgments, jealousy, fear, and anger—none of these choices will lead you to peace. Making such ego-driven choices can become habitual, but, as we have established, no habit is sacrosanct. If you really want peace in your life (and who would deny the attraction to peaceful lives?), before doing anything you must carefully evaluate the action, with the help of your Higher Power. Before speaking, taking any action, even before planning a future activity, it's wise to stop and examine what you are about to do. If the choice you are considering is not conducive to a peaceful experience, it's best to choose again.

Discovering the avenue to peace isn't really very difficult if your search is serious. It's a one-way street, in fact. Peace is the byproduct of loving thoughts and kind actions. If we are thinking the thoughts God would want us to think and acting the way God would want us to act, we will experience peace. It will wash over us like a warm wave. The people who are on the receiving end of our loving actions and kind thoughts will experience a wave of the peace we are feeling too.

Let's examine this idea more closely. A loving thought might be a prayer for understanding or for forgiveness. It might be a prayer for the well-being of an adversary or for one who is ill. It might be a nonspecific prayer on behalf of the troubled world. A loving thought might simply be recognizing the "holiness" of every encounter. Being willing to shift one's perspective whenever a conflict has arisen is a loving thought. It's a shift that doesn't even have to be verbalized to the parties present to it. Doing it will register on the situation anyway, and it will be felt. Acknowledging one's gratitude for the present moment and all past moments, too, is an expression of a loving thought. Recognizing that the anger of anyone is a byproduct of fear, and sending him or her quiet, prayerful thoughts of peace, is what God would have us do.

Loving, kind actions are not mysterious either. Perhaps the one that is easiest and comes first to mind is smiling rather than frowning whenever an opportunity to do one or the other presents itself. Surrendering to a situation that you cannot control or to a person who is adamant that his or her opinion is right is a kind action. Don't misunderstand. Surrendering doesn't mean letting someone walk all over you; it only means that you would rather be peaceful than caught in the maze of "rightness." Being right is always a matter of perspective. Fighting to win a point will never cultivate a feeling of peace.

Actually walking away from an encounter that is ugly is making the kinder choice. It defuses the situation, and it demonstrates that there is another way to interact. Let me go a few steps further. We do not need to argue, ever. We do not need to defend our perspective, ever. We do not need to force our opinion on others, ever. Disagreements don't require resolution, but keeping disagreements alive will never make room for the peace we so deserve.

Changing your mind from agitated to peaceful requires little effort, really. You can begin by taking a deep breath before responding to any situation. Then just invite God into the moment. Every time you avail yourself of this simple two-step approach, you create more peace, not only in your own life but in the lives of everyone else, too. Each one of us can have an impact; the world changes as our minds change. One decision, one choice at a time.

Be Willing to Ask Yourself, "Would I Rather Be Peaceful Or Right?"

I have raised this idea before, but let's focus on it for a moment. The number of times per day that you have the opportunity to choose between being peaceful or "right" probably falls into the hundreds. On many of these occasions, it is not an easy choice. You may feel personally committed to one side of an issue or the other, and bowing out of the discussion or walking away feels like abandoning your position. You can choose to shift your perspective, however, and see that when you walk away you are, in actuality, making a choice that benefits everyone in the discussion. By choosing not to rail until the bitter end, you can allow both sides to walk away with their dignity intact.

One's ego is frequently so intent on pushing its point that we end up in discussions we don't even need to be having, many of them heated, and over issues we don't really care about. Apparently we have been trained to think that we have to finish whatever deliberation we are a part of, but that is not the case. Not continuing a discussion to its bitter end is such a freeing decision. Our "adversaries" might try to guilt us into continuing the discussion, particularly if they think they are close to convincing us that they are right, but they have no control over our decision to leave the discussion. The choice is ours and we'll never find peace if we stay in discussions that are heated and that have no chance for a happy resolution.

The desire for peaceful relationships seems to gain in importance the older we get. I certainly have a past replete with heated arguments over issues I often knew nothing about. But I was intent on being right, on forcing others to give in, hopefully forcing them to finally agree that my position was the right one. I think my insecurities fed my compulsion to be right. I have no interest in doing this anymore. Not because I don't have opinions on issues nor because I don't feel committed to a personal philosophy. It's because my peace of mind has become more important to me than winning an argument—any argument—and experiencing the agitation that comes with disagreements no longer fuels my body with the energy I need for further engagement.

As always, there is a much larger issue at stake here than just the individual choice of peace over being right. Every time we make a peaceful choice we add to the peace of the world. This may not seem possible, but think about it. When you feel respected, don't you tend to radiate that good feeling to others as well? And when you are confronted by hostility, doesn't that tend to stress you and color your next interactions? Each response any one of us makes multiplies exponentially. When we choose a peaceful response, the effect of our choice radiates outward into the world.

Not getting entangled in other people's dramas or trying to ensnare people in ours, particularly if that's been our longtime pattern, is just wonderfully freeing. This one step, choosing to be peaceful rather than right, takes lots of practice, but it pays huge dividends toward a peaceful life and a peaceful world.

Become Willing—That's All It Takes

Willingness is what allows for a change of mind. Simple willingness. Such a gentle word, never forceful or controlling. Being willing is simply making a commitment to approach new situations from a position of possibility rather than expectation, to be willing to release an old idea or opinion in favor of keeping an open mind. It invites us to be contemplative before making the decisions that matter to us.

Our resistance to releasing old ideas or opinions can feel positively overpowering. Our old ways of doing and thinking served us well, or so we think. At least we knew what to expect! But what many of us fail to appreciate is that being unwilling to entertain a fresh perspective means not allowing the voice of our Higher Power to play a part in our decisions, our opinions, our perceptions of others in the present moment. We may have let Him/Her help us in the past, perhaps with the very decisions we still cling to, but now we are stuck, unwilling to make room for a fresh, more fitting perspective. This happens because the ego tends to take control of the old idea, make it its own, and "whip us" with it. To paraphrase a line from *A Course in Miracles*, the ego speaks first, is loudest, and is always wrong.

Where does willingness to open our minds to the voice of our Higher Power come from? Actually, it is always available to us; it just doesn't draw attention to itself. It stands in the wings, waiting for us to invite it to center stage. Bringing it forth is actually not difficult at all. It's a matter of remaining vigilant to our own thoughts and ensuring that whatever action we have in mind will not be hurtful to anyone else. Of course the ego can be very sneaky and interfere with our plans almost without our noticing. Some say it can even mimic the voice of our Higher Power. That's why we have to get quiet, extremely quiet, to make sure we know whom we are hearing. Remember the title of this chapter: There are two voices in your mind, and one is always wrong! Choose carefully.

Each Day the Process for Change Can Begin Again

I'll never forget the first time I saw a poster that said, in big, bold letters: One day at a time. I couldn't fathom what it even meant. But then a kind person explained it to me—and I was relieved. Trying to imagine doing anything, especially

Change Your Mind and Your Life Will Follow

something difficult, for the rest of our lives can immobilize us. But we can imagine doing it one day at a time. And that's all we need to do. I know that I certainly could not imagine changing the pattern of my alcohol and drug use for the rest of my life, but I felt I could refrain from using these substances one day at a time. And that idea gave me the courage to give it a try. I am suggesting we use the same method for changing our minds and our lives. Few of us can promise we will never again resort to an old pattern of thinking or behaving for the duration of a lifetime. But giving ourselves the option to make the promise each day, and only for that day, makes it quite manageable to change a behavior or attitude or opinion that is no longer benefiting us. We only have to become willing to let the God of our understanding participate in all our decisions on a moment-by-moment basis. Each moment, each hour, each day that we let God participate through our willingness to listen to His/Her voice, we will be far more peaceful, and we will help to initiate peace in the lives of others too.

Each morning upon arising we are free to make this commitment willingly to listen and then follow the guidance if we so choose. Doing so cultivates a feeling of hope that our lives can become a reflection of our fondest dreams. However, seldom are we initially eager to change, no matter how much sense the change makes. Change always means unfamiliarity, at least for a time. And very few of us are comfortable with the unfamiliar. Therefore some days we resist. That's okay, too.

Continuing along the old path of thinking and behaving is like walking in comfy slippers. They might be wearing out, but until the soles are gone, we don't want to discard them. And we don't have to. Nor do we have to listen every day to God. No one but us is in charge of our willingness to do anything.

That's why our goal is to commit to making a change for one day only, and only when we want to. To most people this seems manageable. You can even reduce your focus to changing just one experience at a time, if that makes it easier to muster up your willingness.

The whole idea here is to be free to do only as much changing as you want to do, and only when you want to do it. No one is watching over your shoulder. No one cares, really, how and when or if you change a behavior, an attitude, or an opinion. The main beneficiary of our changes is us.

One day at a time. What a concept. There is nothing we can't do if we do it in small enough increments. Since we are certain of being alive only one instant at a time, let's cherish the awareness that right now we can begin our day again with a new idea, a new attitude, and the appropriate accompanying behaviors. Anytime you choose to begin is the right time. Take it slow and small and your life will change.

When You Begin Is Up to You

I think it's safe to assume that no one likes to live a chaotic life. No one enjoys being in a state of constant judgment or agitation. Being trapped in arguments of our own making or letting the behavior of others control our thoughts and actions is certainly no fun either. Yet some of us live in one (or several!) of these states for a long time because we are afraid of changing our behavior, or because we are unaware that we have the power to change our minds as well as our actions, or because we don't realize there is help available for changing whatever we may want to change.

Our lives can be so much simpler than we make them. For instance, we don't need to do anything alone. We don't need to take responsibility for anyone else. Turning our lives and minds, and the lives of everyone else too, over to the loving care of a Higher Power would change every experience, every expectation, and every relationship we have. Our lives would certainly look very different if this were the case.

But no one has set a timetable for changing your life. If you are interested in having a more joyful or more peaceful life, you get to choose when to start. There may be no time like the present, but that doesn't mean you have to do it now. In actuality, you don't ever have to do it! The loving voice will wait for your invitation for as long as necessary. When you finally want to change your life, it will join your effort.

CHAPTER 13

Shortcuts for Changing Our Minds and Our Lives—A Summary

As you have seen, none of the ideas in this book is all that complicated or mysterious. Many of the concepts were probably familiar to you, in fact, particularly if you are already traveling a spiritual path. But it has been my experience that it can be extremely helpful to review and reinforce such powerful ideas, if only to remind us and affirm us in staying the course. Then, of course, comes practice. Nothing changes if nothing changes. So if these ideas appeal to you, I hope you will commit to incorporating some of them, or eventually all of them, into your life.

Remember, you don't have to make big changes all at once. A tiny change adhered to will be just as effective, if not more so, than a large one only practiced half-heartedly. This final chapter is all about finding those small changes that you can make—one day at a time. We'll be reviewing the many suggestions already made in the first twelve chapters but looking at how to take them in bite-sized pieces. No one can or should change an entire life overnight. But, and this idea is at the very heart of this book, we don't have to. Every one of us is capable of choosing new thoughts, which will lead to new behaviors, one thought, one behavior at a time. And thus our lives will change. The changes will not go unnoticed by the people we touch. That's the additional benefit.

So, let's review:

Cultivating New Behaviors

Live and Let Live

Releasing ourselves from the affairs of others is a profoundly freeing experience. It means we can achieve our own goals. It means we can focus on practicing the principles of peaceful living wherever we go. It simplifies our lives and makes us available to do the work that God has chosen for us to do, the work we agreed to do before our arrival here.

Live and let live doesn't mean living without caring about other people. It just means getting out of their way; it means approaching every interaction from the perspective that we are in one another's lives for the purpose of learning specific lessons. In every interaction we are exchanging information. Every encounter gives us an opportunity to be of help to one another but not to control. Coming from this perspective, we can approach our social interactions as both teacher and student. But taking charge of others, or trying to, is never one of the assignments. How lucky we are that this is true.

Turn Your Focus from Problem to Solution

Whatever we focus on multiplies. When we focus on a problem, we exacerbate it. It's something like having a toothache. Even the tiniest problem will become monumental if we give it our constant attention. The beauty of being human is that we have a choice. We don't have to focus on problems; we can open our minds to solutions. This is a major shift in perspective, and its first step is willingness—the simple willingness to shift our focus away from the problem. By taking this first step, we open the door to the problem's resolution. Sometimes it's downright spooky how resolutions appear once we allow ourselves to see them.

The truth of the matter is that most of our biggest "problems" in life are not life-threatening; rather, they are little more than ordinary situations that we choose to complicate. Quite often it is our way of reacting or overreacting that fuels the tiny flame, and before we know it a full-fledged fire is under way. But we can keep the fire from spreading if we become willing to see how our own behavior contributed to its growth and then make the decision to back off, way off, from the whole situation.

A common example that comes to mind is a simple disagreement with a significant other over the plans for a birthday celebration. If I (or you) insist that the party be a surprise and very costly, and I "win" the argument, I must be aware that the event may well have lost its joyful tenor. No one gains when such a thing occurs.

The fact is, we always have the choice to turn from a problem focus to a resolution focus. We get to choose how big we want to make a problem. We don't have to do things the way we've always done them. This is a huge revelation for many of us. We can disengage from any situation. We can say nothing or simply walk away. A great beginning is simply to see problems as opportunities to let God into our lives. Take it from me. The sense of personal empowerment that accompanies letting God handle the problem while we attend to watching for the solution is life-changing.

Let me say it again. The so-called problems in our lives are largely the work of our interfering egos. Remember what I said earlier about the two voices in our heads, the ego and the quiet voice of peace. The ego always speaks loudest, and it is always wrong. It thrives on the chaos of unsolved problems. God lives in the peaceful solution. It's our choice which voice we will listen to.

Let Go

You'll recall our earlier discussion about how we are responsible only for making the effort, not for the outcome. Sounds good, right? The problem is that taking our hands off a situation, after making the effort that is ours to make, is not easy. We want to be in charge of the outcome too because of how it will impact our lives, particularly our security, but it is not ours to control and never was.

Trying to be in charge of outcomes, which are always uncontrollable, means we are never done with our work, never disengaged from situations or people. Not only is this exhausting, sometimes beyond measure, but it also means we are taking responsibility away from others, too. Just as important as doing only our work is letting other people do theirs. It takes time and practice to be able to walk away when the time is right, but it is a choice that is always ours to make.

When our minds are on the past or the future, which is where they tend to go when we are trying to control outcomes, we often experience agitation or anxiety, sometimes both, but seldom peace. We cannot be an example of peace except in each present moment. And we can't know peace unless we experience God's presence, which is always available, moment by moment. Our job is to show up for it.

With practice, we can learn to let the past call without going there. We can also learn to let the future beckon without moving toward it. Planning for the future, which is not a bad idea, does not mean living there ahead of time. There are so many opportunities for letting go. Practicing any one of them will benefit us in all the rest of them too.

Experience a Miracle

The phrase "as you think, so you are" is key to understanding the control we have over how our lives are unfolding. If we are not happy with the outcome so far, the choice to have a happier life is ours. You see, our lives match our thoughts. We are in charge of our thoughts as well as their creation. Whatever thought we are harboring, whatever perception we are nurturing, was handpicked. That's the bad news. But any thought that troubles us can be discarded. It's our choice. That's the good news. And how refreshing.

Not being stuck with any thought that doesn't promote peace is very good news indeed. It gives every one of us a chance to have a positive impact on every person and situation we experience, because just as our peaceful thoughts comfort us, they also comfort others. The question for some of us is: How do we discard the thoughts that keep us resentful or fearful, or full of shame and guilt, or angry and separated from others? These thoughts seem to cling to us like glue. But the truth of the matter is, we cling to them.

We cling to thoughts that injure us or others because they are familiar. Changing even one thought will have consequences we cannot predict nor plan for, and that's simply too uncomfortable to bear. Whatever reality we have lived with will change just as soon as our thoughts change. And we are the only ones who can change the picture we see.

The only thing standing in the way of our enjoying the peace we deserve is our resistance to choosing another thought when the one we are protecting is doing us or others harm. This simple act of shifting our perception can exponentially add to the peace of the world.

Act, Don't React

Many of us have become quite masterful at letting other people determine our feelings, either through their perceptions of us or their actions, or both. We allow other people's actions toward us to engender in us a thoughtless reaction or self-conscious withdrawal. But we can refrain from either response, regardless of the circumstances, regardless of what the other person has said or done. Remember the John Powell story? That many of us have spent years under the overt or covert domination of others is grievous, but there is still time for a happy life.

That happy life begins with taking charge of our actions. It means making the choice to act rather than react to the whims of others. You know as well as I do that our quick reaction is usually wrong. It's almost always the better path to take the extra moment to consider our response to others and to life, and to act rather than react. In that extra moment we have the opportunity to hear God's soft voice, and every time we make the decision to listen to the softer voice we will be able to refrain from reacting. God's soft voice will guide us to do the loving thing, to speak the kind words, to walk away from the situations that are escalating into ugly scenes.

Being able to act rather than react to any person, place, or thing is only as hard as we make it. If we always do what we always did, nothing in our life will change. However, if we dare to walk a different walk and talk a different talk, nothing will remain the same. The choice is always dangling before us.

Drop Your Judgments—Judgments and Love Cannot Coexist

Judgments are a poison to us and all our relationships. They come from the ego, and they are very cunning, baffling, and powerful. And most of us are so accustomed to making them that we take no notice of them much of the time, and when we do, we justify them by saying that we are simply sharing our opinion, or being painfully honest in an attempt to be helpful or in order to clarify situations or improve them. The ego may be very clever, but we don't have to be fooled.

Judgments imprison us in the way they monopolize our feelings, our actions, our plans, our hopes and dreams. Every time we sit in judgment of another person, our lives are diminished; they become narrower. We need to ask ourselves why we continue to do something that has such a detrimental impact on our own lives.

Being judgmental is a habit, and it can be changed.

With effort and the help of our Higher Power, we can see that our judgments are a reflection of how we see ourselves and the fear that consumes us. Seeking help and forgiveness for our own shortcomings is one pathway to being free of the judgments we so easily and often gleefully make about others.

Training ourselves to feel and then express unconditional love, the antidote to judgment, is possible, particularly with God's help. We can choose to bring God into our minds whenever we find ourselves in the act of judging; this changes our experience and our perspective instantly. Practicing gratitude is another simple way to escape from the habit of being judgmental.

Let's try to remember that we choose all our relationships for the lessons they bring. Being willing to accept these lessons and the people who bring them can change our minds from judgment to love and acceptance. Our fears, which push us to judge, have no power over us if we keep God and gratitude and willingness and acceptance in the forefront of our minds. The willingness to change our minds is the all-powerful solution to all disharmony in our lives.

Our minds are never idle! Let's choose our thoughts lovingly and carefully and with God as our guide.

Accept Your Powerlessness— It's the Greatest Gift

Abandoning our attempts to control other people is a profound form of personal liberation. It's not easy to do, however, even after years of trying. Our fears make us cling to the idea that if we can control others, our own lives will be more content. We assume that our security and well-being are directly tied to the behavior of others; therefore, the more focused we are on controlling their behavior, the happier we will be. Only after practicing the process of letting go of what others do, over a period of months or even years, will we be able to see how our lives are not, nor were they ever, secure or content as the result of someone else's actions. Our lives become peaceful and secure in direct proportion to our awareness of the unconditional love of God.

Every person alive has a chosen journey, one that is right for him or her. Letting the truth of this sink in is one way to begin the process of giving up control, as is acknowledging that the more we try to control someone, the less interested he or she may be in staying in our life. Every time we get into a power struggle with the person we are trying to control, we drive a wedge into the relationship. Other people's desire to escape will be directly proportional to our continuing obsession with how they are living and what they are doing.

Another reason that we try to keep other people attached to us through control is to avoid our feelings of insecurity and inadequacy. Feeling threatened unless we are constantly being validated because others are acquiescing to our control is what keeps us stuck and unable to complete the journey we are actually here to make. Those unhelpful feelings must be relinquished, and can be, if we remember and appreciate the idea that we are all teachers and students, here to learn from one another but never to control one another.

Our choice is to live in harmony or disharmony. Few of us would consciously choose the latter. However, if we cling to unpeaceful thoughts—and every attempt to control someone else is an unpeaceful thought—we can never experience the peace we so deserve. There is an easier, softer way. Why not choose it?

Be the Center of Your Own Attention

Our lives reflect our thoughts, and when our thoughts are consumed by our attention on others, we miss the many opportunities and lessons that are beckoning to us. "Codependency" is a popular term for this obsession. Living through the lives of others—watching others' every move to discover who we are and the depth of our acceptability—is a lonely place to live. It's also a path that doesn't allow us to participate in the events we had "requested" to experience in this life.

Our obsessions with other people's lives prevent us from fulfilling our own purpose, which in turn creates in us a sense of insignificance, which then feeds our obsession. Quite the vicious circle.

The good news is, it is altogether possible to share in each other's lives without having the boundaries between us blurred. We can walk side by side, helping one another along the way. We can be supportive, loving, affirming, and grateful for the "partnership." And we can celebrate the control we are limited to: control over our own minds and lives, control over the effort we put in a relationship, control over the gratitude we choose to feel on a daily basis, and control over the decision to open our minds to the constant presence of God, who is always waiting to show us the way to a more peace-filled life.

Such a life can only be attained in one way. The choice to seek it is as close as the next thought.

Do No Harm

There are so many ways of doing harm. Some seem quite minor and call on our utmost vigilance. Not listening, not responding, not making eye contact, being discounting, responding with a growl, and perhaps the most common, criticism, might be slight but they are nonetheless harmful. When anyone anywhere is diminished by our treatment, we have done harm. Verbal, physical, and sexual abuse, the forms of harm we commonly think of, are in reality just a tiny percentage of the harm committed all around us all the time.

And the fact is, all of humanity is harmed by our arguments. We tend to respond in kind to the treatment we receive, and thus our harmful actions and reactions multiply, and likewise their aftereffects. Furthermore, every harmful act is covering fear.

Fortunately it's never too late to be a more loving presence in another person's life. The fact is, we always have the choice to be kind, unflinchingly compassionate, or loving. If we are not feeling kind or loving, we may occasionally choose no action at all. That's a far better choice than hurting someone. But the best choice is always to refrain from injuring another person, and it's not such an extraordinary choice unless you think it is, nor does this decision to never harm another person have to be made more than once unless we are inclined to let our ego get in the way of our heart's better judgment. In those situations where our egos have reigned supreme, thankfully we can choose again.

If it seems unreasonable to commit to doing no harm forever, do it for just one day. Anybody can take control of his or her actions for one day. The payoff for every kindness we offer is immediate, and it coaxes us to consider being kind again and again. Every time we choose to be loving and helpful, every time we choose to sidestep an inclination to hurt someone, our lives improve. We become a reflection of our actions. That's just a fact. Those individuals who spend their time cultivating loving thoughts toward others experience far more loving lives.

We can always choose the high road when dealing with other people. Regardless of what their behavior may be, we don't have to reciprocate in kind. Just for today we can do anything. Just for today we can be the people we know God wants us to be. A great rule of thumb is to ask oneself, before making any comment or taking any action: "Is what I am about to say or do going to please God?"

The Dalai Lama story that was shared earlier is a great and simple reminder of our responsibility here. He said simply and eloquently, "Love one another. And if you can't love one another, at least don't hurt one another." The right choice is obvious. Are you willing to make it?

Quiet Your Mind and Hear God's Voice

Beneath the noisy voice of the ego lies the quiet voice of God. We can only hear this quiet voice by emptying or silencing our busy, chattering minds. And that's not so very easy. The average person probably entertains thousands of thoughts daily. Pushing any thought aside to make room for the quiet voice of one's Higher Power is a choice we don't always want to make, particularly if we are in a punishing mood. Harboring anger or fear or resentments gives us the illusion of power and control, making our inclination to cling to them very strong. It's not until we have experienced the peace and freedom of releasing all mean-spirited thoughts that we have any idea how different our lives can feel.

Accepting responsibility for our every thought doesn't always make us proud. Try monitoring your thoughts for just an hour. The ego is never quiet. It's always comparing, contrasting, criticizing, arguing, resenting, and trying to control.

It's never doing anyone a worthwhile service. Its very existence is fueled by being allowed to create and strengthen only the most hurtful ideas, which are generally followed by behaviors that match them. Bad thoughts evolve into bad behaviors. The news is not all bad, of course. We are not hostage to our thoughts. We can choose to release any thought at any moment, and when we do we will see our lives begin to change. Any thought we have can be traded for a better one, and peaceful, loving thoughts energize us. After experiencing both, those who really want to make a positive difference in the lives of others and themselves will think carefully before harboring any thought that doesn't reflect the will of God. We must never forget that what we put out there comes back to us. Accepting responsibility for our part in this equation empowers us. We can change our minds and our lives will follow! Peaceful thoughts make peaceful people, and peaceful people promise all of us a more peaceful world.

Every Encounter Is a Holy Encounter

I have always found this idea very reassuring. It means I don't have to be in constant turmoil about God's will. If I accept the premise that no one is on my path accidentally and that everyone is a child of God, I am more willing to accept their presence and the circumstances that have brought us together. My acceptance allows me to respond respectfully, even in those situations where love is not forthcoming. If neither feels possible, I can remain silent.

I also find that embracing the idea that no encounter outranks any other encounter makes it easier to navigate through all of them. Some encounters may not feel as easy or joyful or loving as others, but that does not diminish their value or their necessity. All of them were "preselected," and are part of the unfolding of your life. Gratitude for this does not come naturally; we must develop it.

Is it really possible to look into the eyes of everyone we meet and recognize the holiness of the Spirit within? It's certainly worth making the attempt. In fact I believe it's our most important assignment, the one that will help make this a more peaceful world. And while the world is being transformed, each one of us will experience a personal transformation. It really can't get any better than that.

There Are Two Voices in Your Mind, and One Is Always Wrong—Choose Carefully

By now you are familiar with this idea that we have two voices in our mind always vying for our attention, and that one is always wrong. The interesting question for most of us is: Why do we so often choose to listen to the wrong voice? We have already established that it speaks the loudest. It's also often the most familiar. But I think we pick this voice because it's the one that elevates us at the expense of other people, and that's a place we like to be. It's the one that keeps us feeling separate from others, which feels familiar. And it's also the one that needs our adherence for its survival. Of course it's going to make a pest of itself. It has no other option.

The question we must always ask ourselves is whether we want to harbor agitation, anger, fear, and certain inferiority, or whether we want to experience peace. The choice is ours. The voice for peace will wait for our acknowledgment. Because the peaceful voice belongs to our Higher Power, we can count on it to remain with us always. It doesn't leave our minds even though it's so often ignored. It knows that we will eventually want more peaceful lives, and it will show us the way.

Listening for the softer, quieter voice of God makes every relationship in our lives more fruitful and more peaceful. And the peace we cultivate can be passed on to others too, through our prayers, through our willingness to shift our perceptions, through our decision to surrender our need to be right whenever we are in disagreement with a loved one, a stranger, or a good friend. Passing on our peaceful feelings increases the level of our own peace.

It's common knowledge that all acts of aggression lead to more aggression. All we have to do is watch the news and read the daily papers to prove that point. But we don't always get it that the reverse is also true: acts of love lead to more love, in our own lives as well as those lives we touch. Our one "little act" of love is not meaningless. Far from it. Our lives and the world around us are changed by a multitude of little acts of love—something as simple as a smile or a kind word or a willingness to listen.

How we acquire better lives is not very mysterious. It comes back to making better choices, beginning with the most important choice of all: Whom will we listen to, the aggressive boss ego or the quiet, wise voice that's always there to guide us to a higher place? You don't have to make huge changes all at once. I wouldn't even suggest trying. Just commit, one day at a time, to changing your mind, and you will begin to experience the peaceful life you deserve. The power of one mind changing cannot be overstated. Are you willing to be an example?

This brings me to the end of a wonderful experience. I have been so enriched by the process of writing this book. That's how it always is. My own life improves every time I share with another person those bits of wisdom I have acquired over the years. Choosing to live a peaceful life by making peaceful responses, one response at a time, has given me a feeling of balance and freedom I could never have imagined, and I'm so pleased to share what I have learned with you.

I mentioned earlier that as I age I am less inclined to have to prove a point, any point. I am more willing to surrender and be happy, instead of needing to be right. Perhaps this is what happens to all people as they age. I can't speak for others. But I do know that the more peacefully I respond to the people around me, the more likely I will be loved in return. Isn't that what we really all seek? I think so, and I am going to keep being an example wherever I am. May you find the peace you so richly deserve, and may you remember that even a little change of mind will assuredly change your life. Make it happen.

ABOUT THE AUTHOR

Karen Casey, winner of a 2007 Johnson Institute America Honors Recovery Award for her contributions to the field, is a sought-after speaker at recovery and spirituality conferences throughout the country. She has written thirty-one books, among them *Peace a Day At a Time*, *52 Ways to Live the Course in Miracles*, *20 Things I Know For Sure*, *Codependence and the Power of Detachment*, and this one, *Change Your Mind and Your Life Will Follow*—a bestselling book that is the basis for her Change Your Mind Workshops—plus many more. Her renowned bestseller *Each Day a New Beginning: Daily Meditations for Women*, originally published in 1982, has sold more than 4 million copies and been translated into ten different languages.

Karen Casey divides her time between Minnesota and Florida. To learn more about her work , visit her at www. womens-spirituality.com or at her Facebook page: Karen Casey, Author

Mango Publishing, established in 2014, publishes an eclectic list of books by diverse authors—both new and established voices—on topics ranging from business, personal growth, women's empowerment, LGBTQ+ studies, health, and spirituality to history, popular culture, time management, decluttering, lifestyle, mental wellness, aging, and sustainable living. We were named 2019 *and* 2020's #1 fastest-growing independent publisher by *Publishers Weekly*. Our success is driven by our main goal, which is to publish high-quality books that will entertain readers as well as make a positive difference in their lives.

Our readers are our most important resource; we value your input, suggestions, and ideas. We'd love to hear from you— after all, we are publishing books for you!

Please stay in touch with us and follow us at:

Facebook: Mango Publishing
Twitter: @MangoPublishing
Instagram: @MangoPublishing
LinkedIn: Mango Publishing
Pinterest: Mango Publishing
Newsletter: mangopublishinggroup.com/newsletter

Join us on Mango's journey to reinvent publishing, one book at a time.

CPSIA information can be obtained
at www.ICGtesting.com
Printed in the USA
JSHW032236150623
43333JS00003B/4